Austen

The Wicked Wit
of

JANE AUSTEN

The
Wicked Wit
of
JANE AUSTEN

Compiled, edited and introduced by

Dominique Enright

MICHAEL O'MARA BOOKS LIMITED

First published in Great Britain in 2002 by
Michael O'Mara Books Limited
9 Lion Yard, Tremadoc Road
London SW4 7NQ

A CIP catalogue record for this book is available
from the British Library

ISBN 1-85479-652-6

1 3 5 7 9 10 8 6 4 2

Designed and typeset by Martin Bristow

Printed and bound in Finland by WS Bookwell, Juva

Contents

Introduction

JANE AUSTEN was born in 1775, the seventh of eight children, six of them boys, to a country parson, George Austen, rector of Steventon in Hampshire, and his wife Cassandra. Jane's eldest brother, James, was ten when she was born: he was to go into the Church, eventually taking over his father's living at Steventon; nine-year-old George was handicapped and did not live with the family; Edward, born in 1767, was adopted by his father's distant cousin and landlord, Thomas Knight, eventually becoming a landowner. Henry was born in 1771; like James, he went to St John's, Oxford, after which he was to sign up as an officer with the Oxfordshire Militia, in time giving up his military career to go into banking – at which he was not a success – and then becoming a clergyman. The fifth child was Cassandra, not quite three when Jane was born; she was followed by Francis (Frank), born in 1774, who went into the navy. Charles was born four years after Jane, in 1779: like Frank, he joined the navy, and, like Frank, ended up Rear-Admiral.

This lively, generally happy family lived in a ramshackle rectory which they shared with a number of boys, pupils of a school run by the Austens, small enough for its pupils to be treated as part of the family. 'The Mansion of Learning', wrote Mrs Austen (who as a child wrote verse good enough to impress her uncle, Theophilus Leigh, Master of Balliol College, Oxford), 'where we study all day. Except when we play' seems to have been a cheerful place to grow up in, with much affection and laughter. The Austen boys were taught by their father along with the other boys; it was surely a matter for regret to Cassandra and Jane that they could not attend the school too – though they must have absorbed a great deal of learning by osmosis. The education of girls at that time was limited, but in 1783, when she was seven, Jane and Cassandra were sent away, with their cousin Jane Cooper, who was slightly older, to a school set up by a Mrs Cawley: this did not last long as they all fell seriously ill. After another year or so at home, they were sent to Mrs La Tournelle's girls' school in Reading; at this easygoing establishment they were taught what was considered the essential basics for young ladies – needlework, French, dancing and the like – and otherwise allowed to do more or less what they wanted. They left in 1786 and spent the rest of their time at home, where their informal education was probably a great deal better than it had been at either school. 'I think I may boast myself, with all possible vanity, the most unlearned and uninformed female that ever dared to be an authoress,' Jane Austen later declared (in a letter to James Stanier Clarke, librarian at Carlton House, who had originally contacted her when it became known to the Prince Regent – later George IV – that she was the author of his favourite novels). As is clear from her books she was far from unlearned and uninformed. She was actually a great deal better educated than many: she was well-read and very articulate – a niece commenting on how grammatical even her spontaneous speech was – she had a reasonable, if idiosyncratic, knowledge of history, and could speak French and a little Italian.

Brought up in an atmosphere of literary intelligence, sur-rounded by bright and noisy schoolchildren and by books of all kinds, an intelligent child could not but learn. Jane read widely and avidly – especially eighteenth-century writers such as Johnson, Goldsmith, Richardson, Fielding, Fanny Burney, Sterne – but she and the rest of her family also happily devoured the lighter novels of the day, novels 'of Terror' and 'of Sentiment' (the equivalents of today's paperback horror and romance) – the absurdity of the plots of the sillier ones (which she parodied in her early spoofs and ridiculed in *Northanger Abbey*) providing a fine source of entertainment for them.

A shy child, Jane spent her early years hiding behind her sister Cassandra, to whom she would remain close all her life. Her mother once commented, 'If Cassandra were going to have her head cut off, Jane would insist on sharing her fate.' Her adult life developed from this – always very close to Cassandra, when they were apart they would keep in touch with letters detailing the gossip and events of the day. Jane always made sure that she found something to amuse her sister with; if her subject matter was not amusing in itself, she contrived to make it so.

Jane Austen died in 1817 aged only forty-one, after an illness – identified by some as Addison's disease, by others as a lymphoma, possibly Hodgkin's disease – against which she fought long and uncomplainingly. She wrote six great novels, four of which were published in her lifetime. Her success as a writer lies in that, although her world was small, what she drew from it, and her insights into the people she encountered, allows her novels to function as microcosms of society at large. The keen comedy of her work continues to be as fresh today as when the novels were first published. Just some of her sharpest, most profound and amusing observations – on human nature, money, marriage, life and society – taken from her early works, novels and letters, are collected here, to inspire laughter, thought – and the odd wry grin of recognition.

'Of events her life was singularly barren: few changes and no great crisis ever broke the smooth current of its course,' wrote Jane Austen's nephew, James-Edward Austen-Leigh. And it has become accepted that Jane Austen led a very dull, sheltered life, a life ignorant of world events and of social deprivations, a life barren of emotions, which she filled by writing books in which nothing much happens, that are a vehicle for sharp, witty comments on the narrow band of society she knew. Unremarkable as her life was, it was no more uneventful than that of most people: true, she never travelled abroad, but she had a large and close-knit immediate family – she was one of eight children – and an even larger extended family, with whom she would often go to stay. She was fond of her many nieces and nephews, to whom she was a joyful and sympathetic companion: 'I have always maintained the importance of aunts,' she once remarked.

From her letters, indeed, it would seem as though her life was a mad social whirl – accounts of balls, visits and parties proliferate, described with a combination of exaggerated fancy and detached amusement. But life was not that cosy: poverty and illness presented an even greater threat – especially to women – than they do today. A middle-class woman was dependent upon her family or her husband. For a woman of any 'gentility' to work for her living was virtually inconceivable – hard times forced some to become, say, governesses, but there was little on offer, and it did mean becoming despised by society. As Elizabeth Watson, in the sadly unfinished novel *The Watsons*, says, 'You know we must marry . . . my father cannot provide for us, and it is very bad to grow old and be poor and laughed at.'

Death added to the general insecurity, being then a much closer presence than it is for the majority of people today – childhood mortality was high, many illnesses now disposed of with a few antibiotics were potentially fatal. Disease was feared then as terrible road accidents are today – but disease came to every family. Thus the attitude to death was more robust than it is today. This is not to say that people minded less; their grief was as great as any – but it was more commonly shared. As a seven-year-old, Jane Austen herself almost died; when she, her sister Cassandra, who was ten, and their eleven-year-old cousin, Jane Cooper, were sent away to board at Mrs Cawley's educational establishment in Oxford, which inexplicably moved to Southampton, they all became seriously ill with an infectious fever. Thanks to Jane Cooper's going against Mrs Cawley's wishes and writing to her mother, they were fetched home; this very probably saved Jane's life, but her aunt, Jane Cooper's mother, who must have caught the disease from the little girls, did die of it. Over the years, other members of Jane Austen's family were to die, and every death was felt by the whole family, who would rally round the bereaved. Cassandra's heart was quietly broken when her fiancé, Tom Fowle, died of yellow fever in the West Indies and thereafter she never even contemplated marriage – did this have a subconscious effect on her sister? Close as she was to Cassandra, Jane cannot fail to have been affected – and perhaps this death encouraged her to exercise caution in affairs of the heart. She might well have been in love with Tom Lefroy, a family friend and suitor – and seems to have expected him to propose, and would probably have accepted – but she did not press the matter when he had to go away, just laughing at herself instead; another young man – met one summer – might have captured her heart, but he died before they could meet again. Was it the memories of these young men, or solidarity with Cassandra, that made her change her mind, when Harris Bigg-Wither, the brother of good friends of hers, proposed to her, and she accepted, only to tell him the next day that she had made a mistake and could not marry him? Perhaps it was his name. Or perhaps she did not want to lose the comparative freedom of her life, now that she was writing seriously, although very much in secret.

Jane Austen's letters to her sister reveal a strong element of whistling past the graveyard in matters of love and death in their assumption of a derisive apparent callousness – jokes can be used to fend off fears: 'At length the day is come on which I am to flirt my last with Tom Lefroy, and when you receive this it will be over. My tears flow at the melancholy idea,' she writes mockingly of herself, following the departure of the young man who, had he stayed any longer, she might well have married. A defence against the tears actually flowing? Or: 'I give you joy of our new nephew, and hope if he ever comes to be hanged it will not be till we are too old to care about it.' Or: 'Mrs Hall of Sherbourne was brought to bed yesterday of a dead child, some weeks before she expected, owing to a fright. I suppose she happened unawares to look at her husband.' Or: 'If Mrs Freeman is anywhere above ground give my best compliments to her.'

Neither was Jane Austen's life that removed from the wider world – it would have taken a dimwit not to be aware of the French Revolution and the Napoleonic wars rumbling in the near distance, for instance, and she kept in constant touch with her army-officer brother and with her two naval-officer brothers on their travels. In addition, her older cousin, friend and, later, sister-in-law, Eliza Hancock, who led a much more cosmopolitan life, which she described in lively letters, was married to a French officer, the Comte de Feuillide, who was guillotined by the Committee for Public Safety during the Reign of Terror. Whether it was because she did not feel that she was qualified to comment on current affairs or because they were distasteful to her, or for some other reason, Jane Austen simply chose not to write about these subjects: '3 or 4 families in a country village is the very thing to work on,' she wrote to her niece Anna, seeing in these few representative families, mainly country gentry, enough variety, enough of human vanities, frailties and foolishnesses, to reflect universal human traits.

'I have discovered that our great favourite, Miss Austen, is my country-woman . . . with whom mamma before her marriage was acquainted. Mamma says she was then the prettiest, silliest, most affected, husband-hunting butterfly she ever remembers,' novelist and essayist Mary Russell Mitford wrote in a letter in 1814. Could Mamma have been mistaken? She left the district before she married – and her daughter was only twelve years younger than Jane Austen. That as a child, Jane appeared silly and affected is quite possible – giggling, perhaps, over a comic poem she'd just written; or observing the adults around her too intently, taking in every word they subsequently wished they'd not uttered; seeing a joke in what was to them of utmost seriousness. Another acquaintance, Phila Walter, described her when she was about thirteen as 'whimsical and affected'. But 'husband-hunting'? She cannot have been more than eleven years old when Mrs Mitford knew her – however, the young Jane was, perhaps, already writing about husband-hunting butterflies, in the burlesque sketches and humorous poems that she was composing for the amusement of family and friends. Miss Mitford went on to write: 'A friend of mine says that she has stiffened into the most perpendicular, precise, taciturn piece of single-blessedness that ever existed . . .' Allowing for a touch of malice, in Miss Mitford or in her friend, that too could have been partly true – as an adult, a nervous giggle would have to be stifled – and maybe she was nervous in society; or perhaps the occasion bored her – or Miss Mitford's friend bored her . . . There is in any case more than a touch of dryness in her wit, an irony that could be misunderstood or not discerned by the slower-witted. Even so, her early high-spiritedness never did leave her and elements may be found in the latest of her letters and works.

Along with meticulous observation and a keen eye for absurdity, it is this cool, dry irony that characterizes Jane Austen's mature writing. An unrestrained delight in the absurdities of human nature is very evident in her youthful writing, where – often parodying the popular fiction of the day – she allowed herself to be as silly and ridiculous as she wanted, producing innumerable jokey poems and high-spirited stories and skits to entertain her family and friends, or for them to perform. Preposterous as many of them were, however, they already possessed the recognizable spark of Jane Austen's wicked wit, as may be seen in the selection in this book. In her later writing the boisterousness has largely been replaced by wit sometimes so sharp that it is almost unnoticed – but she did not entirely abandon the outrageously comic characters of her early work, merely refined them: Mr Collins in *Pride and Prejudice*, for example, is a caricature of fatuous and obsequious self-importance.

A keen watcher of other people's behaviour, she noted people's mannerisms, and with her alert mind saw easily through weaknesses, pretension and affectation. She greatly enjoyed gossip, jokes and the tales of those who had had more access to the world – the exploits of her military and naval brothers, for instance. Living at the edge of country gentry – her mother was quite 'well connected' – Jane Austen had many opportunities to observe the ways of the well-off and well-born. While she did not always admire their ways, she recognized and understood the power of social position and the security of money all too well – her own family was far from affluent. She disliked the necessity of marriage – and was amused by the unseemly scramble to make a good match – but at the same time understood the benefits of a good marriage. Such social mores and the behaviour they engendered, furnished her with plenty of material for her books. 'Lord, what fools these mortals be,' she sometimes seems to say with Shakespeare's pixie, Robin Goodfellow – but it is too easy to see her novels as merely comic mockery of mankind: there is also a strong moral thread running through them. The arrogant characters are brought down a peg or two; the greedy lose out, the wicked get what they deserve (even if it is no worse than a silly wife gained and a fortune lost), fools and hypocrites are shown to be fools and hypocrites, marriages for money or position, rather than based on love and affection are shown to be empty, assumptions are dismantled.

As to Jane Austen's literary abilities, Walter Scott wrote truly in his *Journal* (of 14 March 1826) when he commented that she 'had a talent for describing the involvements and feelings and characters of ordinary life which is to me the most wonderful I ever met with. The Big Bow-Wow strain I can do myself like any now going; but the exquisite touch, which renders ordinary commonplace things and characters interesting, from the truth of the description and the sentiment, is denied to me.'

In all collections of quotations, from works of fiction in particular, there arises the question – is that the author's own opinion, or that expressed by his or her characters? If it is a view held by the author's character, does that make it the author's view? In an author like Jane Austen, a view may well be expressed ironically, and as her characters are very human – flawed beings rather than all-out baddies – it is not a case of her 'good' characters always expressing views she agrees with, and the 'bad' expressing views that she condemns. Additionally, her own attitude to her characters can be ambivalent: in *Mansfield Park*, for instance, the heroine is Fanny, but it is Mary Crawford, frivolous and capricious, who appears the more attractive person – and is given the best lines. As Jane Austen's brother Henry wrote in his 'Biographical Notice of the Author' prefacing the posthumous publication of *Northanger Abbey* and *Persuasion*, 'Though the frailties, foibles and follies of others could not escape her immediate detection, yet even on their vices did she never trust herself to comment with unkindness.'

To explain the context of every quotation would defeat the purpose of this book – especially as many of Jane Austen's comments may be read and enjoyed out of context, even if altered slightly in meaning – but where it seemed to help, I have occasionally included a brief introductory note, or extended the odd quotation to give a little of the flavour of the setting. On the whole, however, it is soon clear to the discerning reader as to whether some statement is ironic or not. As for the letters . . . Anne Elliot in *Persuasion* recognizes that 'no private correspondence could bear the eye of others', and if some of the quotations from Jane Austen's letters seem quite outrageous, it should be remembered that the letters were addressed to those close to her, usually Cassandra, who would understand what she meant – and whom she was trying to amuse. And they are amusing – as well as giving a fair idea of the kind of life led by women of her class; high-spirited, newsy and gossipy, the letters flit from subject to subject, and back again, with the odd mischievous comment dropped in here and there, to present an engaging portrait of their author and her family.

DOMINIQUE ENRIGHT,
December 2001

Note on the Novels

In the case of the published novels, the dates given are those of first publication: however, the dates do not necessarily reflect when they were written. The dates given for other of JA's writings indicate – as far as it is known – when they were written.

Elinor and Marianne was written in 1795–6, rewritten as *Sense and Sensibility* in 1797–8, revised in 1809, and published in 1811.

First Impressions was written in 1797, rewritten as *Pride and Prejudice* in 1809, and published in 1813.

Mansfield Park was begun in 1811 and published in 1814.

Emma was begun in 1814 and published in 1816.

Susan was begun around 1798 and was sold to a publisher, Richard Crosby, in 1803, who, beyond advertising it, did nothing. JA was only able to buy it back in 1816, when she renamed the heroine Catherine, by which name the book became known, and wrote a prefatory note to it. It was not published until 1818, and under the title *Northanger Abbey*.

Persuasion, begun in 1815, was published in 1818.

The Watsons was begun in 1804, but abandoned in 1805 with George Austen's death. (The father of the Watson sisters in the novel was to die – possibly a reason for JA's abandonment of the novel when her own father died.)

Sanditon was begun in 1817; JA died before she could finish it.

For ease of reading Jane Austen's spelling and her use of capitals have, in general, been standardized, although in a few instances – for example her preference for 'ei', as in 'freindship' – original spellings have been retained for flavour. Her ampersands have been replaced by 'and'.

[17]

Dramatis Personae

Cassandra: Cassandra Austen (1773–1845), JA's sister

Frank: Francis Austen (1774–1865), JA's brother, nearest to her in age

Fanny Knight: (1793–1882), JA's niece, daughter of brother Edward Knight; in 1829 she married Sir Edward Knatchbull

Anna Austen: (1793–1872), JA's niece, daughter of James; she married Ben Lefroy in 1814

Edward Austen-Leigh: (1798–1874), JA's nephew James-Edward Austen-Leigh, son of James, half-brother of Anna

Caroline Austen: (1805–80), JA's niece, daughter of James and sister of Edward

Martha Lloyd: (1765–1843), lifelong friend of the family, who in 1828 became Frank Austen's second wife

James Stanier Clarke: the Prince Regent's librarian at Carlton House

In a Manner Truly Heroick:
Early Exuberances

As a child and young woman Jane Austen wrote as avidly as she read – satirical sketches and burlesques, comic fragments, 'novels' often in epistolary form, light verse . . . most of it poking fun at the more absurd conventions of her time, whether social or literary. A number of these, written during the years between 1787 and 1793, she copied into three notebooks, Volume I covering 1787-90, Volume II 1790–92, and Volume III 1792–3. Many of these pieces she would dedicate to family members or friends with a flamboyant address. *The Beautifull* [sic] *Cassandra: A Novel in Twelve Chapters*, for instance, was, unsurprisingly, dedicated to Cassandra: 'MADAM You are a Phoenix. Your taste is refined, your Sentiments are noble, and your Virtues innumerable. Your Person is lovely, your Figure, elegant, and your Form, majestic. Your Manners are polished, your Conversation is rational and your appearance singular . . .' Some time later, *Catharine* is also dedicated to her: 'MADAM – Encouraged by your warm patronage of *The Beautiful Cassandra*, and *The History of England*, which through your generous support have obtained a place in every library in the Kingdom, and run through threescore Editions, I take the liberty of begging the same Exertions in favour of the following Novel, which I humbly flatter myself, possesses Merit beyond any already published, or any that will ever in future appear, except such as may proceed from the pen of Your Most Grateful Humble Servt. THE AUTHOR'.

Exuberant and nonsensical as many of these early pieces of writing are, in the rough and unsubtle satire may be seen the delicate, sharp irony of the later Jane Austen. She seems particularly to have enjoyed parodying the popular novels of her day – the heroine is a 'picture of perfection', of noble birth (although she might not know it – or this could apply to the hero) and fine feelings; true love is thwarted, fortunes are lost and found, there are very wicked characters – parents or other relatives, often – and unlikely meetings between long-lost relatives; there is a great deal of weeping and swooning. And all this high emotion is shown in its full ludicrous glory.

They said he was sensible, well-informed, and agreeable; we did not pretend to judge of such trifles, but as we were convinced he had no soul, that he had never read *The Sorrows of Werther*, and that his hair bore not the least resemblance to auburn, we were certain that Janetta could feel no affection for him, or at least that she ought to feel none. The very circumstance of his being her father's choice too, was so much in his disfavour, that . . . *that* of itself ought to have been a sufficient reason in the eyes of Janetta for rejecting him.

Love and Freindship, 1790

[Cassandra's] father was of noble birth, being the near relation of the Duchess of —'s Butler.

The Beautifull Cassandra, ?1789

The twelve chapters of The Beautifull Cassandra *are each a sentence long and relate how sixteen-year-old Cassandra whiles away a day. She starts by helping herself to a bonnet her mother, a milliner, has just finished making for a countess and goes out, meets a chance acquaintance or two, catches a hackney coach and orders the driver to take her to Hampstead, changes her mind when they get there and makes him take her back . . .*

[Chapter 4] She then proceeded to a Pastry-cook's, where she devoured six ices, refused to pay for them, knocked down the pastry cook and walked away ...

[Chapter 6] Being returned to the same spot of the same street she had set out from, the coachman demanded his pay ...

[Chapter 7] She searched her pockets over again and again; but every search was unsuccessful. No money could she find. The man grew peremptory. She placed her bonnet on his head and ran away.

The Beautifull Cassandra, ?1789

Gently brawling down the turnpike road,
Sweetly noisy falls the Silent Stream.
'Ode to Pity', 1787/90

[Elfrida] flew to Frederic and in a manner truly heroick, spluttered out to him her intention of being married the next day.

Frederic's reply is less than encouraging:

'Damme, Elfrida, *you* may be married tomorrow, but *I* won't.'
  This answer distressed her too much for her delicate constitution. She accordingly fainted and was in such a hurry to have a succession of fainting fits, that she had scarcely patience enough to recover from one before she fell into another.

Frederic and Elfrida, 1787/90

But lovely as I was, the graces of my person were the least of my perfections. Of every accomplishment accustomary to my sex, I was mistress.

Love and Freindship, 1790

In Lady Williams every virtue met. She was a widow with a handsome jointure and the remains of a very handsome face. Though benevolent and candid, she was generous and sincere; though pious and good, she was religious and amiable, and though elegant and agreeable, she was polished and entertaining.

Jack and Alice, 1787/1790

One fatal swoon has cost me my Life . . . Beware of swoons, Dear Laura. . . . A frenzy fit is not one quarter so pernicious; it is an exercise to the body and if not too violent, is, I dare say, conducive to health in its consequences – run mad as often as you chuse; but do not faint . . .

Love and Freindship, 1790

One evening in December, as my Father, my Mother, and myself were arranged in social converse round our fireside, we were, on a sudden, greatly astonished by hearing a violent knocking on the outward door of our rustic cot.

My Father started – 'What noise is that,' (said he). 'It sounds like a loud rapping at the door' – (replied my Mother). 'It does indeed,'(cried I). 'I am of your opinion; (said my Father) it certainly does appear to proceed from some

uncommon violence exerted against our unoffending door.'
'Yes (exclaimed I) I cannot help thinking it must be somebody who knocks for admittance.'

'That is another point (replied he); we must not pretend to determine on what motive the person may knock – tho' that someone *does* rap at the door, I am partly convinced.'

Here, a second tremendous rap interrupted my Father in his speech, and somewhat alarmed my Mother and me.

Love and Freindship, 1790

[*A coach arrives*] A gentleman considerably advanced in years, descended from it. At his first appearance my sensibility was wonderfully affected, and e'er I had gazed at him a second time, an instinctive sympathy whispered to my heart that he was my grandfather.

Love and Freindship, 1790

Edward's friend and husband of Sophia, Augustus, returns from a solitary walk:

Never did I see such an affecting scene as was the meeting of Edward and Augustus.

'My life! my soul!' (exclaimed the former) 'My adorable angel!' (replied the latter), as they flew into each other's arms. It was too pathetic for the feelings of Sophia and myself – We fainted alternately on a sofa.

Love and Freindship, 1790

[25]

Jane Austen's brother Francis went to sea on board HMS Perseverance *in 1788 not to see his family again for five years. The following year he became Midshipman, and it was sometime after then that his sister sent him her little tale of Mr Harley, a ship's chaplain.*

In half a year he returned and set off in the stage coach for Hogsworth Green, the seat of Emma. His fellow travellers were, A man without a hat, Another with two, An old maid, and a young wife. This last appeared about 17, with fine dark eyes and an elegant shape; in short, Mr Harley soon found out that she was his Emma and recollected he had married her a few weeks before he left England.

'The Adventures of Mr Harley', ?1789/1790

Her eldest brother, the Rev. James Austen, received this little play, The Visit, *in which the ghost of the late grandmother has much to answer for . . .*

LORD FITZGERALD: I am afraid you found your bed too short. It was bought in my grandmother's time, who was herself a very short woman and made a point of suiting all her beds to her own length, as she never wished to have any company in the house . . .

MISS FITZGERALD: Bless me! there ought to be 8 chairs and there are but 6. However, if your Ladyship will but take Sir Arthur in your lap, and Sophy my brother in hers, I believe we shall do pretty well.

MISS FITZGERALD: I am really shocked at crowding you in such a manner, but my grandmother (who bought all the furniture of this room) as she had never a very large party, did not think it necessary to buy more chairs than were sufficient for her own family and two of her particular friends . . .

LORD FITZGERALD: I wish we had any dessert to offer you. But my grandmother in her lifetime, destroyed the hothouse in order to build a receptacle for the turkeys with its materials; and we have never been able to raise another tolerable one.

The Visit, A Comedy in 2 Acts, 1787/90

In Jack and Alice, *Jane Austen has a character lamenting in tones of high tragedy the loss of her governess:*

'Miss Dickins was an excellent governess. She instructed me in the paths of virtue; under her tuition I daily became more amiable, and might perhaps by this time have nearly obtained perfection, had not my worthy preceptoress been torn from my arms, e'er I had attained my seventeenth year. I never shall forget her last words. 'My dear Kitty' she said 'Good night t'ye.' I never saw her afterwards,' continued Lady Williams wiping her eyes. 'She eloped with the butler the same night.'

Jack and Alice, 1787/1790

The birth of her niece – or 'neice' – Fanny in January 1793 inspired Jane Austen's 'Opinions and Admonitions on the conduct of Young Women' (she took her role of Aunt seriously from the very start) and that of another niece, Anna, three months later, her 'Miscellanious [sic] *Morsels'. These she had written, she informed the baby Fanny, tongue firmly in cheek, because 'I think it my particular duty to prevent your feeling as much as possible the want of my personal instructions', adding in her letter to baby Anna, 'You will derive from them very important Instructions, with regard to your Conduct in Life.'*

The slightly bizarre collection includes 'A Letter from a Young Lady, whose feeling being too Strong for her Judgement, led her into the commission of Errors which her Heart disapproved':

Many have been the cares and vicissitudes of my past life . . . and the only consolation I feel for their bitterness is that on a close examination of my conduct, I am convinced that I have strictly deserved them. I murdered my father at a very early period of my life, I have since murdered my mother, and I am now going to murder my sister. I have changed my religion so often that at present I have not an idea of any left. I have been a perjured witness in every public trial for these past twelve years; and I have forged my own will. In short, there is scarcely a crime that I have not committed . . .

'A Tale' about Wilhelminus, who moves into a cottage, but takes with him so many people that he cannot accommodate them and devises the brilliant plan of erecting tents . . .

An ordinary Genius might probably have been embarrassed in endeavouring to accommodate so large a party, but Wilhelminus with admirable presence of mind gave order for the immediate erection of two noble tents in an open spot in the forest adjoining to the house. Their construction was both simple and elegant – a couple of old blankets, each supported by four sticks, gave a striking proof of that taste for architecture and that happy ease in overcoming difficulties which were some of Wilhelminus's most striking virtues.

'The female philosopher: a Letter' – from one 'Arabella Smythe' to her friend (for how long?), Louisa Clarke, in which she describes meeting friends of Louisa's, and, relating her conversation with them, quotes herself:

'Louisa Clarke (said I) is in general a very pleasant girl, yet sometimes her good humour is clouded by peevishness, envy, and spite. She neither wants understanding nor is without some pretensions to beauty, but these are so very trifling, that the value she sets on her personal charms, and the adoration she expects them to be offered, are at once a striking example of her vanity, her pride, and her folly.' So said I, and to my opinion everyone added weight by the concurrence of their own.

'A Tour through Wales – in a Letter from a young Lady':

. . . My Mother rode upon our little pony, and Fanny and I walked by her side or rather ran, for my Mother is so fond of riding fast that she galloped all the way. You may be sure that we were in a fine perspiration when we came to our place of resting. Fanny has taken a great many drawings of the country, which are very beautiful, tho' perhaps not such exact resemblances as might be wished, from their being taken as she ran along . . .

'A Beautiful Description of the Different Effects of Sensibility on Different Minds', in which Melissa is ill – one has to suppose extremely ill – and here is how some of those nearest and dearest to her react:

. . . Sir William is constantly at her bedside. The only repose he takes is on the sopha in the drawing room, where for five minutes every fortnight he remains in an imperfect slumber, starting up every moment and exclaiming 'Oh! Melissa, Ah! Melissa,' then sinking down again, raises his left arm and scratches his head. Poor Mrs Burnaby is beyond measure afflicted. She sighs every now and then, that is about once a week; while the melancholy Charles says every moment 'Melissa how are you?' . . .

And 'The generous Curate', who had many sons – and, it would seem, many large dogs:

. . . The eldest had been placed at the Royal Academy for Seamen at Portsmouth when about thirteen years old, and from thence had been discharged on board of one of the vessels of a small fleet destined for Newfoundland, where his promising and amiable disposition had procured him many friends among the natives, and from whence he regularly sent home a large Newfoundland dog every month to his family . . .

A Great Deal of It Must Be Invention:
History

Although Jane Austen's formal schooling was brief and unsatisfactory, she was far from being the 'most unlearned and uninformed female' she declared herself to be. An intelligent child brought up in the midst of lively scholarship, she absorbed enough learning from books, family, and her parents' school, to hold her own among those who had received many more years of formal education. Perhaps she found contemporary history schoolbooks inadequate – an amalgamation of dull fact and words put into the mouths of the main participants; whatever the case, she completed, just before her sixteenth birthday, her own *History of England*, which consists of short and, as she says, partial (in the sense of 'biased') biographical sketches of kings and queens, with no dates (as she reassures her readers) and family allusions – for instance, in the selection below, she refers to 'one who tho' now but young, already promises to answer all the ardent and sanguine expectations of his relations and friends' – that is, one of her brothers, Frank or Charles.

'It tells me nothing that does not either vex or weary me. The quarrels of popes and kings, with wars or pestilences, in every page; the men all so good for nothing, and hardly any women at all – it is very tiresome: and yet I often think it odd that it should be so dull, for a great deal of it must be invention. The speeches that are put into the heroes' mouths, their thoughts and designs – the chief of all this must be invention . . .'

CATHERINE MORLAND, *Northanger Abbey*, 1818

'Queen Elizabeth,' said Mrs Stanley, who never hazarded a remark on history that was not well founded, 'lived to a good old age, and was a very clever woman.'

Catharine, 1792

A selection, dated 1791, from a distinctly individual view, dedicated to and illustrated by Cassandra Austen:

THE HISTORY OF ENGLAND FROM THE REIGN OF HENRY THE 4TH TO THE DEATH OF CHARLES THE 1ST
By a partial, prejudiced, and ignorant Historian
NB There will be very few dates in this history

HENRY THE 4TH
Henry the 4th ascended the throne of England much to his own satisfaction in the year 1399, after having prevailed on his cousin and predecessor Richard the 2d to resign it to him, and to retire for the rest of his Life to Pomfret Castle, where he happened to be murdered.

HENRY THE 6TH

I cannot say much for this Monarch's sense – nor would I if I could, for he was a Lancastrian. I suppose you know all about the Wars between him and the Duke of York, who was of the right side; if you do not, you had better read some other History, for I shall not be very diffuse in this, meaning by it only to vent my spleen *against*, and show my hatred *to* all those people whose parties or principles do not suit with mine, and not to give information . . . It was in this reign that Joan of Arc lived and made such a row among the English. They should not have burnt her – but they did . . .

EDWARD THE 4TH

This Monarch was famous only for his beauty and his courage, of which the picture we have here given of him, and his undaunted behaviour in marrying one woman while he was engaged to another, are sufficient proofs . . . One of Edward's mistresses was Jane Shore, who has had a play written about her, but it is a tragedy and therefore not worth reading . . .

HENRY THE 8TH

The crimes and cruelties of this prince were too numerous to be mentioned (as this history I trust has fully shown); and nothing can be said in his vindication, but that his abolishing religious houses and leaving them to the ruinous depredations of time has been of infinite use to the landscape of England in general, which probably was a principal motive for his doing it, since otherwise why should a man who was of no religion himself be at so much trouble to abolish one which had for ages been established in the Kingdom?

ELIZABETH

It was the peculiar misfortune of this woman to have had bad ministers – since wicked as she herself was, she could not have committed such extensive mischeif, had not these vile and abandoned men connived at, and encouraged her in her crimes . . . It was about this time that Sir Francis Drake the first English navigator who sailed round the world, lived, to be the ornament of his country and his profession. Yet great as he was, and justly celebrated as a sailor, I cannot help fore-seeing that he will be equalled in this or the next century by one who tho' now but young, already promises to answer all the ardent and sanguine expectations of his relations and freinds, amongst whom I may class the amiable lady to whom this work is dedicated, and my no less amiable self.

EDWARD THE 6TH

As this prince was only nine years old at the time of his Father's death, he was considered by many people as too young to govern, and the late King happening to be of the same opinion, his mother's brother, the Duke of Somerset, was chosen Protector of the realm during his minority . . . He was beheaded, of which he might with reason have been proud, had he known that such was [to be] the death of Mary Queen of Scotland; but as it was impossible that he should be conscious of what had never happened, it does not appear that he felt particularly delighted with the manner of it . . .

CHARLES THE 1ST

. . . The events of this Monarch's reign are too numerous for my pen, and indeed the recital of any events (except what I make myself) is uninteresting to me . . .

Another Stupid Party:
Balls, Gowns and Other Fashions

FORMAL VISITS, balls and other social occasions feature largely in Jane Austen's letters. These took place far more frequently than they do today. In an age long before ready-made home entertainment – like television – became available, those who could afford it, and who had the time and the space, gave parties. Such social gatherings were the recognized means of meeting people – and to young women of the middle and upper classes presented the all-important opportunity of finding young men to marry them, possibly their only hope of continuing the life to which they had been accustomed since birth.

Women like Jane Austen were too intelligent not to see through the frippery and her letters now and again reveal some impatience with it all. Most of the time, however, she is, if detached and slightly sardonic, generally amused: she seems mostly to have enjoyed observing the other people there – and then writing to her sister about them. (Cassandra herself was, presumably, elsewhere and very probably attending other balls, which we have to assume she described to Jane.) But at other times, she is clearly fed up: 'Another stupid party last night; perhaps if larger they might be less intolerable', and in *Persuasion*, she refers to the 'elegant stupidity of private parties'.

All these social get-togethers required special clothes, and descriptions of garments – and the trouble finding what she wanted – abound in the letters. Once more, Jane Austen seems ambivalent: sometimes genuinely interested in the gowns and caps she describes, and at other times impatient – she wishes gowns could be bought ready-made, remarks that her only ambition was that her hair should be tidy – or ironical: her happiness depends on her being able to touch up her hat with black ink; and Cassandra really *must* get flounces . . .

'I remember I met Miss Dudley last spring with Lady Amyatt at Ranelagh, and she had such a frightful cap on, that I have never been able to bear any of them since.' . . .

[After nearly an hour] . . . Camilla came running towards her with great eagerness, and apparently great pleasure –. 'Oh! my dear Catharine,' said she, half out of breath – 'I have such delightful news for you – But you shall guess what it is – We are all the happiest creatures in the world; would you believe it, the Dudleys have sent us an invitation to a ball at their own house –. What charming people they are! I had no idea of there being so much sense in the whole family – I declare I quite dote upon them –.'

Catharine (1792)

Mrs Badcock and two young women were of the same party, except when Mrs Badcock thought herself obliged to leave them to run round the room after her drunken husband. His avoidance, and her pursuit, with the probable intoxication of both, was an amusing scene.

Letter to Cassandra, 12–13 May 1801

Our ball was chiefly made up of Jervoises and Terrys, the former of whom were apt to be vulgar, the latter to be noisy. I had an odd set of partners: Mr Jenkins, Mr Street, Col. Jervoise, James Digweed, J. Lyford, and Mr Biggs, a friend of the latter. I had a very pleasant evening, however, though you will probably find out that there was no particular reason for it.

Letter to Cassandra, 21–3 January 1799

On every formal visit a child ought to be of the party, by way of provision for discourse. In the present case it took up ten minutes to determine whether the boy were most like his father or mother, and in what particular he resembled either, for of course every body differed, and every body was astonished at the opinion of the others.

Sense and Sensibility, 1811

There were very few beauties, and such as there were not very handsome . . . Mrs Blount was the only one much admired. She appeared exactly as she did in September, with the same broad face, diamond bandeau, white shoes, pink husband, and fat neck.

Letter to Cassandra, 20–1 November 1800

'The sooner every party breaks up, the better.'

Mr Woodhouse, *Emma*, 1816

'One cannot have too large a party. A large party secures its own amusement.'

Emma, *Emma*, 1816

We were at a ball on Saturday, I assure you. We dined at Goodnestone, and in the evening danced two country-dances and the Boulangeries [a French dance]. I opened the ball with Edward Bridges; the other couples were Lewis Cage and

Harriet, Frank and Louisa, Fanny and George. Elizabeth played one country-dance, Lady Bridges the other, which she made Henry dance with her, and Miss Finch played the Boulangeries.

In reading over the last three or four lines, I am aware of my having expressed myself in so doubtful a manner that, if I did not tell you to the contrary, you might imagine it was Lady Bridges who made Henry dance with her at the same time that she was playing, which, if not impossible, must appear a very improbable event to you. But it was Elizabeth who danced. We supped there, and walked home at night under the shade of two umbrellas.

Letter to Cassandra, 5 September 1796

There were only twelve dances, of which I danced nine, and was merely prevented from dancing the rest by want of a partner . . .

Letter to Cassandra, 20–1 November 1800

Another stupid party last night; perhaps if larger they might be less intolerable, but here there were only just enough to make one card-table, with six people to look on and talk nonsense to each other. Lady Fust, Mrs Busby, and a Mrs Owen sat down with my uncle to whist, within five minutes after the three old *Toughs* came in, and there they sat, with only the exchange of Adm. Stanhope for my uncle, till their chairs were announced.

Letter to Cassandra, 12–13 May 1801

The elegant stupidity of private parties.

Persuasion, 1818

Mrs Lefroy has just sent me word that Lady Dorchester means to invite me to her ball on January 8, which, though an humble blessing compared with what the last page records, I do not consider as any calamity.

Letter to Cassandra, 28 December 1798

(They had just received news that Frank had been promoted to Commander, and that there was a chance that they might soon see Charles.)

Our ball on Thursday was a very poor one, only eight couple and but twenty-three people in the room; but it was not the ball's fault.

Letter to Cassandra, 21–3 January 1799

On Wednesday morning it was settled that Mrs Harwood, Mary, and I should go together, and shortly afterwards a very civil note of invitation for me came from Mrs Bramston, who wrote I believe as soon as she knew of the ball. I might likewise have gone with Mrs Lefroy, and therefore, with three methods of going, I must have been more at the ball than anyone else. I dined and slept at Deane; Charlotte and I did my hair, which I fancy looked very indifferent, nobody abused it, however, and I retired delighted with my success.

Letter to Cassandra, 1 November 1800

I had the comfort of finding out the other evening who all the fat girls with short noses were that disturbed me at the 1st H. ball. They all prove to be Miss Atkinsons of Enham.

Letter to Cassandra, 30 November–1 December 1800

Your silence on the subject of our ball makes me suppose your curiosity too great for words. We were very well entertained, and could have stayed longer but for the arrival of my list [cloth] shoes to convey me home, and I did not like to keep them waiting in the cold.

Letter to Cassandra, 24 January 1809

I suppose the Ashford ball will furnish something.

Letter to Cassandra, 11–12 October 1813

Yes, I mean to go to as many balls as possible, that I may have a good bargain.

Letter to Cassandra, 9 December 1808

I was very glad to be spared the trouble of dressing and going, and being weary before it was half over.

Letter to Cassandra, 14–15 October 1813

It may be possible to do without dancing entirely. Instances have been known of young people passing many, many months successively, without being at any ball of any description, and no material injury accrue either to body or mind; – but when a beginning is made – when the felicities of rapid motion have once been, though slightly, felt – it must be a very heavy set that does not ask for more.

Emma, 1816

It was a delightful visit; – perfect, in being much too short.

Emma, 1816

Fashionable attitudes

[Fashionable schools] where young ladies for enormous pay might be screwed out of health and into vanity.

Emma, 1816

On visiting such a school in London:

Charlotte Craven . . . looks very well, and her hair is done up with an elegance to do credit to any education. Her manners are as unaffected and pleasing as ever . . . I was shown upstairs into a drawing-room, where she came to me, and the appearance of the room, so totally unschool-like, amused me very much; it was full of modern elegancies, and if it had not been for some naked cupids over the mantelpiece, which must be a fine study for girls, one should never have smelt instruction.

Letter to Cassandra, from London, 20 May 1813

I continue quite well; in proof of which I have bathed again this morning. It was absolutely necessary that I should have the little fever and indisposition which I had: it has been all the fashion this week in Lyme.

Letter to Cassandra, 14 September 1804

It is the fashion to think [Mrs and Miss Holder] both very detestable, but they are so civil, and their gowns look so white and so nice (which, by the bye, my aunt thinks an absurd pretension in this place), that I cannot utterly abhor them.

Letter to Cassandra, 21–2 May 1801

She was nothing more than a mere good-tempered, civil and obliging young woman; as such we could scarcely dislike her – she was only an Object of Contempt.

Love and Freindship, 1790

A FRIVOLOUS DISTINCTION: CAPS, GOWNS, ETC.

Woman is fine for her own satisfaction alone. No man will admire her the more, no woman will like her the better for it. Neatness and fashion are enough for the former, and a something of shabbiness or impropriety will be most endearing to the latter.

Northanger Abbey, 1818

I bought some Japan ink likewise, and next week shall begin my operations on my hat, on which you know my principal hopes of happiness depend.

Letter to Cassandra, 27–8 October 1798

I find great comfort in my stuff gown, but I hope you do not wear yours too often. I have made myself two or three caps to wear of evenings since I came home, and they save me a world of torment as to hair-dressing, which at present gives me no trouble beyond washing and brushing,

Letter to Cassandra, 1–2 December 1798

I cannot determine what to do about my new gown; I wish such things were to be bought ready-made.

Letter to Cassandra, 24–6 December 1798

My black cap was openly admired by Mrs Lefroy, and secretly I imagine by everybody else in the room.

Letter to Cassandra, 24–6 December 1798

Dress is at all times a frivolous distinction, and excessive solicitude about it often destroys its own aim.

Northanger Abbey, 1818

. . . the purchase of a new muslin gown . . . *I* am determined to buy a handsome one whenever I can, and I am so tired and ashamed of half my present stock, that I even blush at the sight of the wardrobe which contains them. But I will not be much longer libelled by the possession of my coarse spot; I shall turn it into a petticoat very soon. I wish you a merry Christmas, but *no* compliments of the season.

Letter to Cassandra, 24–6 December 1798

I am not to wear my white satin cap to-night, after all; I am to wear a Mamalouc cap instead, which Charles Fowle sent to Mary, and which she lends me. It is all the fashion now; worn at the opera, and by Lady Mildmays at Hackwood balls. I hate describing such things, and I dare say you will be able to guess what it is like. I have got over the dreadful epocha of mantuamaking much better than I expected.

Letter to Cassandra, 8–9 January 1799

Though you have given me unlimited powers concerning your sprig, I cannot determine what to do about it . . . I cannot help thinking that it is more natural to have flowers grow out of the head than fruit. What do you think on that subject?

Letter to Cassandra, 11 June 1799

My hair was at least tidy, which was all my ambition.

Letter to Cassandra, 20–1 November 1800

'A simple style of dress is so infinitely preferable to finery. But I am quite in the minority, I believe; few people seem to value simplicity of dress, – show and finery are every thing.'

Mrs Elton, *Emma*, 1816

Mrs Powlett was at once expensively nakedly dressed; we have had the satisfaction of estimating her lace and her muslin; and she said too little to afford us much other amusement.

Letter to Cassandra, 8 January 1801

I learnt from Mrs Tickars's young lady, to my high amusement, that the stays now are not made to force the bosom up at all; *that* was a very unbecoming, unnatural fashion. I was really glad to hear that they are not to be so much off the shoulders as they were.

Letter to Cassandra, 15 September 1813

You really must get some flounces. Are not some of your large stock of white morning gowns just in a happy state for a flounce – too short?

Letter to Cassandra, 14–15 October 1813

Man only can be aware of the insensibility of man towards a new gown.

Northanger Abbey, 1818

I have determined to trim my lilac sarsenet with black satin ribbon just as my China crape is, 6*d.* width at the bottom, 3*d.* or 4*d.*, at top. Ribbon trimmings are all the fashion at Bath, and I dare say the fashions of the two places are alike enough in that point to content *me*. With this addition it will be a very useful gown, happy to go anywhere.

Letter to Cassandra, 5–8 March, 1814

It would be mortifying to the feelings of many ladies, could they be made to understand how little the heart of man is affected by what is costly or new in their attire; how little it is biased by the texture of their muslin, and how unsusceptible of peculiar tenderness towards the spotted, the sprigged, the mull, or the jackonet.

Northanger Abbey, 1818

I am amused by the present style of female dress; – the coloured petticoats with braces over the white spencers and enormous bonnets upon the full stretch, are quite entertaining. It seems to me a more marked *change* than one has lately seen. – Long sleeves appear universal, even as *dress*, the waists short, and, as far as I have been able to judge, the bosom covered.

Letter to Martha Lloyd, from London, 2 September 1814

In a Fine Burst of Literary Enthusiasm:
Books and Writing

A VORACIOUS READER all her life, Jane Austen had read enough to be able to speak with some authority on the novels of her day, laughing at the extremes of the 'gothic' novels – the novels 'of terror and sentiment' that she so enjoyed parodying – and those novels with heroines of unalloyed beauty, virtue and accomplishment ('pictures of perfection'), works that display 'sublimities of intense feeling' and 'the most splendid portraitures of high conceptions, unbounded views, illimitable ardour, indomitable decision'. She stoutly defended novels as affording a 'more extensive and unaffected pleasure' than other literary works, and also praised novels, such as Fanny Burney's *Cecilia, Camilla* or *Evelina* or Maria Edgeworth's *Belinda*, as displaying the 'most thorough knowledge of human nature, the happiest delineation of its varieties, the liveliest effusions of wit and humour', all 'conveyed to the world in the best-chosen language'. To have a novelist and critic like her was a godsend to the many family members who also wrote, and her nieces especially sent her manuscripts to comment and advise upon, which she did seriously, sensibly – don't write about places you don't know she warns Anna, whom she also counsels against using clichés – and diplomatically: 'you need not mind me'.

James Stanier Clarke, librarian at Carlton House, initially wrote to Jane Austen, in 1815, on behalf of the Prince Regent who had discovered that she was the author of those novels he so enjoyed. Like so many who work with books, Mr Clarke could not resist a spot of participation, and subsequently wrote to her suggesting subjects for her next novels. Politely excusing herself on the grounds that she was too ignorant, she declined to follow his recommendations. At the same time, family members were sending her their manuscripts for comment, so, with the excesses of the popular novels of sentiment and terror in mind, and drawing upon Mr Clarke's rather unworkable ideas, Jane Austen produced her satirical *Plan of a*

Novel, combining aspects of popular literature with the kind of advice authors receive from friends and family . . .

Scene to be in the country, Heroine the daughter of a clergyman, one who after having lived much in the world had retired from it and settled in a curacy, with a very small fortune of his own. – He, the most excellent man that can be imagined, perfect in character, temper, and manners – without the smallest drawback or peculiarity to prevent his being the most delightful companion to his daughter from one year's end to the other. – Heroine a faultless character herself, – perfectly good, with much tenderness and sentiment, and not the least wit – very highly accomplished, understanding modern languages and (generally speaking) *everything that the most accomplished young women learn*, but particularly excelling in Music – her favourite pursuit – and playing equally well on the pianoforte and harp – and singing in the first style. Her person quite beautiful – dark eyes and plump cheeks [how JA herself was described]. – Book to open with the description of father and daughter – who are to converse in long speeches, elegant language – and a tone of high serious sentiment. – The father to be induced, at his daughter's earnest request, to relate to her the past events of his life. This narrative will reach through the greatest part of the *first volume* – as besides all the circumstances of his attachment to her mother and their marriage, it will comprehend his going to sea as Chaplain to a distinguished naval character about the Court, his going afterwards to Court himself, which introduced him to a great variety of characters and involved him in many interesting situations, concluding with his opinions on the benefits to result from tithes being done away, and his having buried his own mother (Heroine's lamented grandmother) in consequence of the High Priest of the Parish in which she died refusing to pay her remains the respect due to them. The father to be of a very literary turn, an Enthusiast in Literature, *nobody's enemy but his own* – at the same time most zealous in discharge of his pastoral duties, the model of an exemplary parish priest. – The heroine's friendship to be sought after by a young woman in the same neighbourhood, of talents and shrewdness, with light eyes and a fair skin, but having a considerable degree of wit, Heroine shall shrink from the acquaintance.

From this outset, the story will proceed, and contain a striking variety of adventures. Heroine and her father never above a fortnight together in one place, *he* being driven from his curacy by the vile arts of some totally unprincipled and heartless young man, desperately in love with the Heroine, and pursuing her with unrelenting passion. – No sooner settled in one country of Europe than they are necessitated to quit it and retire to another – always making new acquaintance, and always obliged to leave them. – This will of course exhibit a wide variety of characters – but there will be no mixture; the scene will be for ever shifting from one set of people to another – but all the good will be unexceptionable in every respect – and there will be no foibles or weaknesses but with the wicked, who will be completely depraved and infamous, hardly a resemblance of humanity left in them. – Early in her career, in the progress of her first removals, Heroine must meet with the Hero – all perfection of course – and only prevented from paying his addresses to her by some excess of refinement. – Wherever she goes, somebody falls in love with her, and she receives repeated offers of marriage – which she refers wholly to her father, exceedingly angry that *he* should not be first applied to. – Often carried away by the Anti-hero, but rescued either by her father or by the Hero – often reduced to support herself and her father by her talents, and work for her bread; continually cheated and defrauded of her hire, worn down to a skeleton, and now and then starved to death. – At last, hunted out of civilized society, denied the poor shelter of the humblest cottage, they are compelled to retreat into Kamchatka, where the poor father, quite worn down, finding his end approaching, throws himself on the ground, and after four or five hours of tender advice and parental admonition to his miserable child, expires in a fine burst of literary enthusiasm, intermingled with invectives against holders of tithes. – Heroine inconsolable for some time – but afterwards crawls back towards her former country – having at least twenty narrow escapes from falling into the hands of the Anti-hero – and at last in the very nick of time, turning a corner to avoid him, runs into the arms of the Hero himself, who having just shaken off the scruples which fetter'd him before, was at the very moment setting off in pursuit of her. – The tenderest and completest éclaircissement takes place, and they are happily united. – Throughout the whole work, Heroine to be in the most elegant society and living in high style. The name of the work *not* to be *Emma*, but of the same sort as *S. and S.* and *P. and P.*

Plan of a Novel according to hints from various quarters, 1816

As an inducement to subscribe, Mrs Martin [running the circulating-library] tells me that her collection is not to consist only of novels, but of every kind of literature, etc etc. She might have spared this pretension to *our* family, who are great novel-readers and not ashamed of being so; but it was necessary, I suppose, to the self-consequence of half her subscribers.

Letter to Cassandra, 18–19 December 1798

'I think you must like Udolpho, if you were to read it; it is so very interesting.'

'Not I, faith! No, if I read any, it shall be Mrs Radcliffe's; her novels are amusing enough; they are worth reading; some fun and nature in them.'

'Udolpho was written by Mrs Radcliffe,' said Catherine, with some hesitation, from the fear of mortifying him.

CATHERINE MORLAND and JOHN THORPE,
Northanger Abbey, 1818

We had a Miss North and a Mr Gould of our party; the latter walked home with me after tea. He is a very young man, just entered of Oxford, wears spectacles, and has heard that *Evelina* was written by Dr Johnson.

Letter to Cassandra, 2 June 1799

Catherine . . . in rather a solemn tone of voice, uttered these words, 'I have heard that something very shocking indeed will soon come out in London.'

[*Eleanor Tilney understandably imagines something terrible, but:*] . . . 'My dear Eleanor, the riot is only in your own brain. The confusion there is scandalous. Miss Morland has been talking of nothing more dreadful than a new publication which is shortly to come out, in three duodecimo volumes, two hundred and seventy-six pages in each, with a frontispiece to the first, of two tombstones and a lantern–do you understand?'

CATHERINE MORLAND and HENRY TILNEY,
Northanger Abbey, 1818

Because they were fond of reading, she fancied them satirical: perhaps without exactly knowing what it was to be satirical; but that did not signify.

Sense and Sensibility, 1811

Provided that nothing like useful knowledge could be gained from them, provided they were all story and no reflection, she had never any objection to books at all.

Northanger Abbey, 1818, of Catherine Morland

'But you never read novels, I dare say?'

'Why not?'

'Because they are not clever enough for you – gentlemen read better books.'

'The person, be it gentleman or lady, who has not pleasure in a good novel, must be intolerably stupid.'

Catherine Morland and Henry Tilney,
Northanger Abbey, 1818

'I am no indiscriminate novel-reader. The mere trash of the common circulating library, I hold in the highest contempt. You will never hear me advocating those puerile emanations which detail nothing but discordant principles incapable of amalgamation, or those vapid tissues of ordinary occurrences from which no useful deductions can be drawn. – In vain may we put them into a literary alembic; – we distil nothing which can add to science. – You understand me I am sure?'

Sir Edward, *Sanditon*, 1817

[Sir Edward:] 'The novels which I approve are such as display human nature with grandeur – such as show her in the sublimities of intense feeling – such as exhibit the progress of strong passion from the first germ of incipient susceptibility to the utmost energies of reason half-dethroned, – where we see the strong spark of woman's captivations elicit such fire in the soul of man as leads him . . . to hazard all, dare all, achieve all, to obtain her. – Such are the works which I peruse with delight, and I hope I may say, with amelioration. They hold forth the most splendid portraitures of high conceptions, unbounded views, illimitable ardour, indomitable decision – and even when the Event is mainly anti-prosperous to the high-toned machinations of the prime character, the potent, pervading Hero of the Story, it leaves us full of generous emotions for him; – our hearts are paralysed. – 'Twere Pseudo-Philosophy to assert that we do not feel more enwrapped by the brilliancy of his career, than by the tranquil and morbid virtues of any opposing character . . . These are the novels which enlarge the primitive capabilities of the heart, and which it cannot impugn the sense, or be any dereliction of the character, of the most anti-puerile man to be conversant with.'

'If I understand you aright,' said Charlotte, 'our taste in novels is not at all the same.'

Sanditon, 1817

I will not adopt that ungenerous and impolitic custom so common with novel writers, of degrading by their contemptuous censure the very performances, to the number of which they are themselves adding – joining with their greatest enemies in bestowing the harshest epithets on such works, and scarcely ever permitting them to be read by their own heroine, who, if she accidentally take up a novel, is sure to turn over its insipid leaves with disgust. Alas! If the heroine of one novel be not patronized by the heroine of another, from whom can she expect protection and regard? I cannot approve of it. Let us leave it to the reviewers to abuse such effusions of fancy at their leisure, and over every new novel to talk in threadbare strains of the trash with which the press now groans. Let us not desert one another; we are an injured body. Although our productions have afforded more extensive and unaffected pleasure than those of any other literary corporation in the world, no species of composition has been so much decried.

Northanger Abbey, 1818

Fond as she is of gothic novels, Catherine's good sense overrides her imagination and she misses her cue to swoon . . .

He looked as handsome and as lively as ever, and was talking with interest to a fashionable and pleasing-looking young woman, who leant on his arm, and whom Catherine immediately guessed to be his sister; thus unthinkingly throwing away a fair opportunity of considering him lost to her forever, by being married already . . . and therefore, instead of turning of a deathlike paleness and falling in a fit on Mrs Allen's bosom, Catherine sat erect, in the perfect use of her senses.

Northanger Abbey, 1818

The truth was that Sir Edward, whom circumstances had confined very much to one spot, had read more sentimental novels than agreed with him.

Sanditon, 1817

We have tried to get *Self-Control*, but in vain. I *should* like to know what her estimate is, but am always half afraid of finding a clever novel *too clever*, and of finding my own story and my own people all forestalled.

Letter to Cassandra, 30 April 1811

Jane Austen eventually found Self-Control, *a novel by a Mrs Brunton, and was relieved to find its heroine a 'picture of perfection'.*

[I will write] a close imitation of *Self-Control* as soon as I can; – I will improve upon it; – my heroine shall not merely be wafted down an American river in a boat by herself, she shall cross the Atlantic in the same way and never stop till she reaches Gravesend.

Letter to Anna Lefroy (Austen), late 1814/early 1815

To her niece Anna, Jane Austen wrote about characters in a novel that Anna was then writing, teasing her about her new husband Ben:

I wish you would not let him plunge into a 'vortex of dissipation'. I do not object to the thing, but I cannot bear the expression; it is such thorough novel slang, and so old that I dare say Adam met with it in the first novel he opened.

Letter to Anna Lefroy (Austen), 28 September 1814

His having been in love with the aunt gives . . . an additional interest . . . I like the idea – a very proper compliment to an aunt! I rather imagine indeed that nieces are seldom chosen but out of compliment to some aunt or another. I dare say Ben was in love with me once, and would never have thought of you if he had not supposed me dead of a scarlet fever.

Letter to Anna Lefroy (Austen), 30 November 1814

If people like to read their books, it is all very well, but to be at so much trouble in filling great volumes, which, as I used to think, nobody would willingly ever look into, to be labouring only for the torment of little boys and girls, always struck me as a hard fate.

CATHERINE MORLAND, *Northanger Abbey*, 1818

I am very much obliged to you for sending your MS. It has entertained me extremely; all of us indeed. I read it aloud to your Grandmama and Aunt Cass., and we were all very much pleased.

. . . If *you* think differently, however, you need not mind me. I am impatient for more . . .

I *do* think you had better omit Lady Helena's postscript. To those that are acquainted with *Pride and Prejudice* it will seem an imitation.

. . . and we think you had better not leave England. Let the Portmans go to Ireland; but as you know nothing of the manners there, you had better not go with them. You will be in danger of giving false representations. Stick to Bath and the Foresters. There you will be quite at home.

Letter to Anna Austen, 10 August 1814

I am quite determined however not to be pleased with Mrs West's *Alicia de Lacy* [*an Historical Romance*], should I ever meet with it, which I hope I may not. – I think I *can* be stout against anything written by Mrs West. – I have made up my mind to like no novels really, but Miss Edgeworth's, yours and my own.

Letter to Anna Austen, 9–18 September 1814

How good Mrs West [a prolific authoress] could have written such books and collected so many hard works, with all her family cares, is still more a matter of astonishment! Composition seems to me impossible with a head full of joints of mutton and doses of rhubarb.'

Letter to Cassandra, 8–9 September 1816

Walter Scott has no business to write novels, especially good ones. It is not fair. He has fame and profit enough as a poet, and should not be taking the bread out of the mouths of other people.

Letter to Anna Austen, 28 September 1814

Fanny and the two little girls . . . revelled last night in *Don Juan*, whom we left in Hell at half-past eleven. . . . The girls . . . still prefer *Don Juan*; and I must say that I have seen nobody on the stage who has been a more interesting character than that compound of cruelty and lust.

Letter to Cassandra from London, 15–16 September 1813

'Oh! It is only a novel!' replies the young lady, while she lays down her book with affected indifference, or momentary shame. 'It is only *Cecilia*, or *Camilla*, or *Belinda*'; or, in short, only some work in which the greatest powers of the mind are displayed, in which the most thorough knowledge of human nature, the happiest delineation of its varieties, the liveliest effusions of wit and humour, are conveyed to the world in the best-chosen language.

Northanger Abbey, 1818

I do not wonder at your wanting to read *First Impressions* again, so seldom as you have gone through it, and that so long ago.

Letter to Cassandra, 9 January 1799

I would not let Martha read *First Impressions* again upon any account, and am very glad that I did not leave it in your power. She is very cunning, but I saw through her design; she means to publish it from memory, and one more perusal must enable her to do it.

Letter to Cassandra, 11 June 1799

*(*First Impressions *was the original title of* Pride and Prejudice*; JA was of course not serious about Martha.)*

'A person who can write a long letter with ease, cannot write ill.'

MISS BINGLEY, *Pride and Prejudice*, 1813

I am very much flattered by your commendation of my last letter, for I write only for fame, and without any view to pecuniary emolument.

Letter to Cassandra, 14–15 January 1798

I could no more write a [historical] romance than an epic poem. I could not sit seriously down to write a serious romance under any other motive than to save my life, and if it were indispensable for me to keep it up and never relax into laughing at myself or other people, I am sure I should be hung before I had finished the first chapter.

Letter to James Stanier Clarke, 1 April 1816

'MY OWN DARLING CHILD'

No, indeed, I am never too busy to think of *S. and S.* I can no more forget it than a mother can forget her sucking child.

Letter to Cassandra, 25 April 1811

[. . .] I want to tell you that I have got my own darling child [*Pride and Prejudice*] from London.

Letter to Cassandra, 29 January 1813

Lady Robert is delighted with *P. and P.*, and really *was* so, as I understand, before she knew who wrote it – for, of course, she knows now. He [Henry] told her with as much satisfaction as if it were my wish.

Letter to Cassandra, 15–16 September 1813

Poor Dr Isham is obliged to admire *P. and P.*, and to send me word that he is sure he shall not like Madame D'Arblay's [Fanny Burney's] new novel half so well. Mrs Cooke invented it all, of course.

23–4 September 1813

I dined upon goose yesterday, which, I hope, will secure a good sale of my second edition [of *Sense and Sensibility*].

Letter to Cassandra, 11–12 October 1813

Since I wrote last, my 2nd edit. [of *Sense and Sensibility*] has stared me in the face . . . I cannot help hoping that *many* will feel themselves obliged to buy it. I shall not mind imagining it a disagreeable duty to them, so as they do it.

Letter to Cassandra, 6–7 November 1813

Henry has this moment said that he likes my *M[ansfield] P[ark]* better and better; – he is in the third volume. I believe *now* he has changed his mind as to foreseeing the end; he said yesterday, at least, that he defied anybody to say whether H[enry] C[rawford] would be reformed, or would forget Fanny in a fortnight.

Letter to Cassandra, 5–8 March 1814

Perhaps before the end of April, *Mansfield Park* by the author of S & S – P & P may be in the world. – Keep the *name* to yourself, I should not like to have it known beforehand.

Letter to Frank, 21 March 1814

In addition to their standing claims on me they admire *Mansfield Park* exceedingly. Mr Cooke says 'it is the most sensible novel he ever read' and the manner in which I treat the clergy delights them very much.

Letter to Cassandra, 14 June 1814

You will be glad to hear that the first edition of *M[ansfield] P[ark]* is all sold. Your uncle Henry is rather wanting me to come to town to settle about a second edition, but as I could not very conveniently leave home now, I have written him my will and pleasure, and, unless he still urges it, shall not go. I am very greedy and want to make the most of it, but as you are much above caring about money I shall not plague you with any particulars.

Letter to Fanny Knight, 18–20 November 1814

Make everybody at Hendon admire *Mansfield Park*.

Letter to Anna Lefroy (Austen), 22 November 1814

I am strongly haunted with the idea that to those readers who have preferred *Pride and Prejudice*, [*Emma*] will appear inferior in wit, and to those who have preferred *Mansfield Park* inferior in good sense.

Letter to James Stanier Clarke, 11 December 1815

I am quite concerned for the loss your mother mentions in her letter. Two chapters and a half to be missing is monstrous! It is well that *I* have not been at Steventon lately, and therefore cannot be suspected of purloining them; – two strong twigs and a half towards a nest of my own would have been something. – I do not think however that any theft of that sort would be really very useful to me. What should I do with your strong, manly, spirited sketches, full of variety and glow? – How could I possibly join them on to the little bit (two inches wide) of ivory on which I work with so fine a brush, as produces little effect after much labour?

Letter to eighteen-year-old Edward Austen-Leigh,
16–17 December 1816

Let other pens dwell on guilt and misery. I quit such odious subjects as soon as I can, impatient to restore everybody, not greatly in fault themselves, to tolerable comfort, and to have done with all the rest.

Mansfield Park, 1814

Uncle Henry writes very superior sermons. – You and I must try to get hold of one or two, and put them into our novels; – it would be a fine help to a volume; and we could make our heroine read it aloud on a Sunday evening, just as well as Isabella Wardour, in the Antiquary, is made to read the History of the Hartz Demon in the ruins of St Ruth, though I believe, on recollection, Lovell is the reader.

Letter to eighteen-year-old Edward Austen-Leigh,
16–17 December 1816

I have just received nearly twenty pounds myself on the second edition of *Sense and Sensibility* which gives me fine flow of literary ardour.

Letter to Caroline Austen, 14 March 1817

Do not be surprised at finding Uncle Henry acquainted with my having another ready for publication. I could not say No when he asked me, but he knows nothing more of it. You will not like it, so you need not be impatient. You may *perhaps* like the heroine, as she is almost too good for me.

Letter to Fanny Knight, 23-5 March 1817

(The novel was Persuasion.*)*

Fanny – 'You are the oddest creature! Quite unrepulsible, hardened and impudent,' exclaimed her aunt – had made one of her suitors, James Wildman, read one or more of Jane Austen's novels, without divulging the author's identity, and had pressed him for his comments, which she then passed on to her aunt.

I . . . do not think the worse of him for having a brain so very different from mine. . . . Do not oblige him to read any more. Have mercy on him . . . He and I should not in the least agree, of course, in our ideas of novels and heroines; – pictures of perfection, as you know, make me sick and wicked . . . I particularly respect him for wishing to think well of all young ladies; it shows an amiable and a delicate mind. – And he deserves better treatment than to be obliged to read any more of my works.

Letter to Fanny Knight, 23-5 March 1817

I must make use of this opportunity to thank you dear Sir, for the very high praise you bestow on my other novels – I am too vain to wish to convince you that you have praised them beyond their merit . . . I am quite honoured by your thinking me capable of drawing such a clergyman . . . – A classical education, or at any rate, a very extensive acquaintance with English Literature, ancient and modern, appears to me quite indispensable for the person who would do any justice to your clergyman – I think I may boast myself, with all possible vanity, the most unlearned and uninformed female that ever dared to be an authoress.

Letter to James Stanier Clarke, 11 December 1815

The Rich are
Always Respectable

P*lus ça change* . . . but for women of Jane Austen's class at the end of the eighteenth century and beginning of the nineteenth, money was additionally important – women like her were not expected to go out to work – or, rather, were expected not to go out to work. So, if they did not inherit or marry money they were in trouble. It was certainly a worry to Jane Austen – who, however, viewed it with her customary irony.

'Business, you know, may bring money, but friendship hardly ever does.'

MR JOHN KNIGHTLEY, *Emma*, 1816

This morning brought me a letter from Mrs Knight, containing the usual fee, and all the usual kindnesses. She asks me to spend a day or two with her this week . . . I sent my answer . . . which I wrote without much effort, for I was rich – and the rich are always respectable, whatever be their style of writing.

Letter to Cassandra, 20–22 June 1808

(Mrs Knight, adoptive mother of JA's brother Edward, seems to have taken it upon herself to pay JA a regular allowance.)

I find, on looking into my affairs, that instead of being very rich I am likely to be very poor . . . as we are to meet in Canterbury I need not have mentioned this. It is as well, however, to prepare you for the sight of a sister sunk in poverty, that it may not overcome your spirits.

Letter to Cassandra, 24 August 1805

Given an introduction to a neighbour, JA and Frank went to visit the lady:

We found only Mrs Lance at home, and whether she boasts any offspring besides a grand pianoforte did not appear . . . They will not come often, I dare say. They live in a handsome style and are rich, and she seemed to like to be rich, and we gave her to understand that we were far from being so; she will soon feel therefore that we are not worth her acquaintance.

Letter to Cassandra, 7–8 January 1807

People get so horridly poor and economical in this part of the world that I have no patience with them. Kent is the only place for happiness; everybody is rich there.

Letter to Cassandra, 18–19 December 1798

I am tolerably glad to hear that Edward's income is so good a one – as glad as I can be at anybody's being rich except you and me – and I am thoroughly rejoiced to hear of his present to you.

Letter to Cassandra, 8–9 January 1799

'An annuity is a very serious business; it comes over and over every year, and there is no getting rid of it.'

MRS JOHN DASHWOOD, *Sense and Sensibility*, 1811

'A large income is the best recipe for happiness I ever heard of. It certainly may secure all the myrtle and turkey part of it.'

MARY CRAWFORD, *Mansfield Park*, 1814

'Money can only give happiness where there is nothing else to give it.'

MARIANNE DASHWOOD, *Sense and Sensibility*, 1811

P. and P. is sold. – Egerton gives £110 for it. – I would rather have had £150, but we could not both be pleased, and I am not at all surprised that he should not choose to hazard so much.

Letter to Martha Lloyd, 29–30 November 1812

I was previously aware of what I should be laying myself open to – but the truth is that the Secret has spread so far as to be scarcely the shadow of a secret now – and that I believe that whenever the third appears, I shall not even attempt to tell lies about it. – I shall rather try to make all the money than all mystery I can of it.

Letter to Frank, 25 September 1813

'But if you observe, people always live for ever when there is an annuity to be paid them.'

MRS JOHN DASHWOOD, *Sense and Sensibility*, 1811

'After all that romancers may say, there is no doing without money.'

ISABELLA THORPE, *Northanger Abbey*, 1818

'A single woman, with a very narrow income, must be a ridiculous, disagreeable, old maid! the proper sport of boys and girls; but a single woman, of good fortune, is always respectable, and may be as sensible and pleasant as anybody else.'

EMMA, *Emma*, 1816

A Truth
Universally Acknowledged:
The Marriage Market

A CRITICISM regularly aimed at Jane Austen's novels is that their main concern is marriage. While it is true that marriage forms the basis of every plot, some critics have allowed the irritation and contempt this fact seems to have aroused in them to blind them to the author's wit and the irony with which she views social life. Ralph Waldo Emerson is positively splenetic: '. . . vulgar in tone, sterile in artistic invention, imprisoned in the wretched conventions of English society, without genius, wit, or knowledge of the world. Never was life so pinched and narrow,' he splutters. 'The one problem in the mind of the writer . . . is marriagebleness.'

It might be fairer to say that Jane Austen saw marriagebleness as a problem in the life of so many young women of her class. That it was necessary to marry if a woman wanted to avoid a life of poverty she recognized but did not like. Worst of all was if a girl could not find a husband in her social circle and whose family could not support her. For then she had either to support herself by becoming, say, a teacher – and that could not have paid more than just enough to keep her in a state of respectable but shabby gentility – or be shipped out like a cargo to India and elsewhere to be chosen – or not – by the unmarried young British men sent abroad to seek their fortunes or to keep out of their families' hair. But even if she could find a husband, it was wrong, very wrong, in Jane Austen's eyes to marry without at least affection, if not love. She is emphatic about this, even fiercely romantic, while remaining clear-eyed enough to know that in real life, where the woman was so often dependent upon the man for her livelihood, her ideal of love on both sides and a nice fortune to boot was a matter of chance. But at least she could make something very like it happen in her novels. In the meantime, she could mock the ridiculous lengths to which young women, and even more their mothers, would go to secure 'good' marriages.

It is a truth universally acknowledged, that a single man in possession of a good fortune must be in want of a wife.

Pride and Prejudice, 1813

However little known the feelings or views of such a man may be on his first entering a neighbourhood, this truth is so well fixed in the minds of the surrounding families, that he is considered as the rightful property of some one or other of their daughters.

Pride and Prejudice, 1813

Commenting on one of the characters in a novel her niece had written, Jane Austen remarks:

What he says about the madness of otherwise sensible women on the subject of their daughters coming out is worth its weight in gold.

Letter to Anna Austen, 18 August 1814

Mr Collins had only to change from Jane to Elizabeth, and it was soon done – done while Mrs Bennet was stirring the fire.

Pride and Prejudice, 1813

'Almost as soon as I entered the house, I singled you out as the companion of my future life. But before I am run away with by my feelings on this subject, perhaps it would be advisable for me to state my reasons for marrying – and moreover for coming into Hertfordshire with the design of selecting a wife, as I certainly did.'

MR COLLINS, Pride and Prejudice, 1813

'Oh, Mr Bennet, you are wanted immediately; we are all in an uproar. You must come and make Lizzy marry Mr Collins, for she vows she will not have him, and if you do not make haste he will change his mind and not have her.' . . .

'I have not the pleasure of understanding you,' said he, when she had finished her speech. 'Of what are you talking?'

'Of Mr Collins and Lizzy. Lizzy declares she will not have Mr Collins, and Mr Collins begins to say that he will not have Lizzy.' . . .

'Come here, child,' cried her father as she appeared. 'I have sent for you on an affair of importance. I understand that Mr Collins has made you an offer of marriage. Is it true?' Elizabeth replied that it was. 'Very well – and this offer of marriage you have refused?'

'I have, sir.'

'Very well. We now come to the point. Your mother insists upon your accepting it. Is not it so, Mrs Bennet?'

'Yes, or I will never see her again.'

'An unhappy alternative is before you, Elizabeth. From this day you must be a stranger to one of your parents. Your mother will never see you again if you do not marry Mr Collins, and I will never see you again if you do.'

Pride and Prejudice, 1813

It would be an excellent match, for *he* was rich, and *she* was handsome.

Sense and Sensibility, 1811

Without thinking highly either of men or of matrimony, marriage had always been [Charlotte Lucas's] object; it was the only honourable provision for well-educated young women of small fortune, and however uncertain of giving happiness, must be their pleasantest preservative from want.

Pride and Prejudice, 1813

'But you know we must marry . . . but my father cannot provide for us, and it is very bad to grow old and be poor and laughed at.'

ELIZABETH WATSON, *The Watsons*, 1804

But there certainly are not so many men of large fortune in the world as there are pretty women to deserve them.

Mansfield Park, 1814

'Pray, my dear aunt, what is the difference in matrimonial affairs, between the mercenary and the prudent motive? Where does discretion end, and avarice begin?'

ELIZABETH BENNET, *Pride and Prejudice*, 1813

'It is a manoeuvring business. I know so many who have married in the full expectation and confidence of some one particular advantage in the connexion, or accomplishment, or good quality in the person, who have found themselves entirely deceived, and been obliged to put up with exactly the reverse. What is this but a take-in?'

MARY CRAWFORD, Mansfield Park, 1814

'She is not the first girl who has gone to the East Indies for a husband, and I declare I should think it very good fun if I were as poor.'

CAMILLA, Catharine, 1792

Single women have a dreadful propensity for being poor – which is one very strong argument in favour of matrimony.

Letter to Fanny Knight, 13 March 1817

'Happiness in marriage is entirely a matter of chance.'

CHARLOTTE LUCAS, Pride and Prejudice, 1813

In all the important preparations of the mind [Maria Bertram] was complete: being prepared for matrimony by an hatred of home, restraint, and tranquillity; by the misery of disappointed affection, and contempt of the man she was to marry.

Mansfield Park, 1814

To Mr Woodhouse, 'hating change of every kind,':

Matrimony, as the origin of change, was always disagreeable.
Emma, 1816

'In nine cases out of ten, a woman had better show *more* affection than she feels.'
CHARLOTTE LUCAS, *Pride and Prejudice*, 1813

'In marriage especially . . . there is not one in a hundred of either sex who is not taken in when they marry. Look where I will, I see that it *is* so; and I feel that it *must* be so, when I consider that it is, of all transactions, the one in which people expect most from others, and are least honest themselves.'
MARY CRAWFORD, *Mansfield Park*, 1814

The public . . . is rather apt to be unreasonably discontented when a woman does marry again, than when she does not.
Persuasion, 1818

'An engaged woman is always more agreeable than a disengaged. She is satisfied with herself. Her cares are over, and she feels that she may exert all her powers of pleasing without suspicion. All is safe with a lady engaged; no harm can be done.'
HENRY CRAWFORD, *Mansfield Park*, 1814

That numerous class of females, whose society can raise no other emotion than surprise at there being any men in the world who could like them well enough to marry them.

Northanger Abbey, 1818

When any two young people take it into their heads to marry, they are pretty sure by perseverance to carry their point, be they ever so poor, or ever so imprudent, or ever so little likely to be necessary to each other's comfort.

Persuasion, 1818

'I pay very little regard to what any young person says on the subject of marriage. If they profess a disinclination for it, I only set it down that they have not yet seen the right person.'

Mrs Grant, *Mansfield Park*, 1814

On the subject of matrimony, I must notice a wedding in the Salisbury paper, which has amused me very much, Dr Phillot to Lady Frances St Lawrence. *She* wanted to have a husband I suppose, once in her life, and *he* a Lady Frances.

Letter to Cassandra, 24–5 October 1808

'It is always incomprehensible to a man that a woman should ever refuse an offer of marriage. A man always imagines a woman to be ready for any body who asks her.'

Emma, *Emma*, 1816

'Let him have all the perfections in the world, I think it ought not to be set down as certain that a man must be acceptable to every woman he may happen to like himself.'

FANNY, *Mansfield Park*, 1814

'A lady's imagination is very rapid; it jumps from admiration to love, from love to matrimony in a moment.'

MR DARCY, *Pride and Prejudice*, 1813

'You could not have made me the offer of your hand in any possible way that would have tempted me to accept it.'

ELIZABETH BENNET, *Pride and Prejudice*, 1813

'I had not known you a month before I felt that you were the last man in the world whom I could ever be prevailed on to marry.'

ELIZABETH BENNET, *Pride and Prejudice*, 1813

Happily [Mr Woodhouse] was not farther from approving matrimony than from foreseeing it. – Though always object-ing to every marriage that was arranged, he never suffered beforehand from the apprehension of any; it seemed as if he could not think so ill of any two persons' understanding as to suppose they meant to marry till it were proved against them.

Emma, 1816

Your news of Edward Bridges was *quite* news, for I have had no letter from Wrotham. – I wish him happy with all my heart, and hope his choice may turn out according to his own expectations, and beyond those of his family – and I dare say it will. Marriage is a great improver ... As to money, that will come, you may be sure, because they cannot do without it.

Letter to Cassandra, 20 November 1808

'People that marry can never part, but must go and keep house together. People that dance only stand opposite each other in a long room for half an hour.'

CATHERINE MORLAND, *Northanger Abbey*, 1818

Lady Sondes' match surprises, but does not offend me; had her first marriage been of affection, or had there been a grown-up single daughter, I should not have forgiven her; but I consider everybody as having a right to marry *once* in their lives for love, if they can, and provided she will now leave off having bad headaches and being pathetic, I can allow her, I can *wish* her, to be happy.

Letter to Cassandra, 27–8 December 1808

Miss Bigg ... writes me word that Miss Blachford *is* married. But I have never seen it in the paper. And one may as well be single, if the wedding is not to be in print.

Letter to Anna Lefroy (Austen), late February/
early March 1815

'And to marry for money I think the wickedest thing in existence.'

CATHERINE MORLAND, *Northanger Abbey*, 1818

A good man must feel, how wretched, and how unpardonable, how hopeless, and how wicked it was to marry without affection.

Mansfield Park, 1814

'Poverty is a great evil; but to a woman of education and feeling it ought not, it cannot be the greatest. I would rather be a teacher at a school (and I can think of nothing worse) than marry a man I did not like.'

EMMA WATSON, *The Watsons*, 1804

Anything is to be preferred or endured rather than marrying without affection.

Letter to Fanny Knight, 18 November 1814

Nothing can be compared to the misery of being bound *without* love, bound to one, and preferring another.

Letter to Fanny Knight, 30 November 1814

The Nature of their Attachments:
Men and Women

AND MATRIMONY means men and women and the relationships between them. Intellectually, the male and female characters in Jane Austen's novels are shown as equals, foolish or wise, clever or stupid – but it is nevertheless tacitly understood that ultimately the man is the boss. Naive Catherine – interestingly, a tomboy just a few years before, who preferred cricket to dolls ('she was fond of all boy's plays . . . noisy and wild, hated confinement and cleanliness, and loved nothing so well in the world as rolling down the green slope at the back of the house': could this have been the young Jane Austen?) – believes that men don't read novels because such books are 'not clever enough for you – gentlemen read better books'. But, although she is not as feisty as Elizabeth Bennet, it is Anne Elliot in *Persuasion* who comes nearest to a protest against the situation of women: 'We live at home, quiet, confined, and our feelings prey upon us. You are forced on exertion. You have always a profession, pursuits, business of some sort or other, to take you back into the world immediately, and continual occupation and change soon weaken impressions.' On the whole, however, Jane Austen's heroines are well able to hold their own with men, and verbally at least quite often have the upper hand.

'One cannot be always laughing at a man without now and then stumbling on something witty.'

ELIZABETH BENNET, *Pride and Prejudice*, 1813

'I never heard a young lady spoken of for the first time without being informed that she was very accomplished.'

MR BINGLEY, *Pride and Prejudice*, 1813

'I have sometimes thought,' said Catherine, doubtingly, 'whether ladies do write so much better letters than gentlemen! That is – I should not think the superiority was always on our side.'

'As far as I have had opportunity of judging, it appears to me that the usual style of letter-writing among women is faultless, except in three particulars.'

'And what are they?'

'A general deficiency of subject, a total inattention to stops, and a very frequent ignorance of grammar.'

CATHERINE MORLAND and HENRY TILNEY,
Northanger Abbey, 1818

'If there is anything disagreeable going on men are always sure to get out of it.'

MARY MUSGROVE, *Persuasion*, 1818

'I never in my life saw a man more intent on being agreeable than Mr Elton. It is downright labour to him where ladies are concerned. With men he can be rational and unaffected, but when he has ladies to please, every feature works.'

JOHN KNIGHTLEY, *Emma*, 1816

'Man is more robust than woman, but he is not longer lived; which exactly explains my view of the nature of their attachments.'

ANNE ELLIOT, *Persuasion*, 1818

'We certainly do not forget you as soon as you forget us.'

ANNE ELLIOT, *Persuasion*, 1818

'I do not think I ever opened a book in my life which had not something to say upon woman's inconstancy. Songs and proverbs, all talk of woman's fickleness.'

MR HARVILLE, *Persuasion*, 1818

'Men have had every advantage of us in telling their own story. Education has been theirs in so much higher a degree; the pen has been in their hands. I will not allow books to prove anything.'

ANNE ELLIOT, *Persuasion*, 1818

'All the privilege I claim for my own sex (it is not a very enviable one; you need not covet it), is that of loving longest, when existence or when hope is gone.'

ANNE ELLIOT, *Persuasion*, 1818

'So, Lizzy . . . your sister is crossed in love, I find. I congratulate her. Next to being married, a girl likes to be crossed in love a little now and then. It is something to think of, and gives her a sort of distinction among her companions.'

MR BENNET, *Pride and Prejudice*, 1813

'Is not general incivility the very essence of love?'

ELIZABETH BENNET, *Pride and Prejudice*, 1813

'But that expression of "violently in love" is so hackneyed, so doubtful, so indefinite, that it gives me very little idea. It is as often applied to feelings which arise from an half-hour's acquaintance, as to a real, strong attachment. Pray, how violent was Mr Bingley's love?'

MRS GARDINER, *Pride and Prejudice*, 1813

'I think very highly of the understanding of all the women in the world – especially of those – whoever they may be – with whom I happen to be in company.'

HENRY TILNEY, *Northanger Abbey*, 1818

'That would be the greatest misfortune of all! – to find a man agreeable whom one is determined to hate!'

ELIZABETH BENNET, *Pride and Prejudice*, 1813

'You are too sensible a girl . . . to fall in love merely because you are warned against it.'

MRS GARDINER, *Pride and Prejudice*, 1813

[Anne Elliot] had been forced into prudence in her youth, she learned romance as she grew older: the natural sequel of an unnatural beginning.

Persuasion, 1818

'If I loved you less, I might be able to talk about it more.'

MR KNIGHTLEY, *Emma*, 1816

There are such beings in the world – perhaps one in a thousand – as the creature you and I should think perfection; where grace and spirit are united to worth, where the manners are equal to the heart and understanding; but such a person may not come in your way, or, if he does, he may not be the *eldest son* of a man of fortune, the near relation of your particular friend, and belonging to your own county.

Letter to Fanny Knight, 18 November 1814

Love, they say, is like a rose;
I'm sure 'tis like the wind that blows,
For not a human creature knows
How it comes or where it goes.
It is the cause of many woes:
It swells the eyes and reds the nose,
And very often changes those
Who once were friends to bitter foes.

From one of the verses to rhyme with 'Rose', 1807

Jane Austen
in Love – and Not

IT IS EASY TO SPECULATE, especially when facts are few. It is known that Jane Austen had a number of suitors, some not at all serious – faintly interested young men who were probably frightened away by her sharpness of mind and ironic, mocking, sense of humour. And some more serious – she seems to have expected, and probably hoped, her relationship with Tom Lefroy, her 'Irish friend . . . for whom I don't care sixpence', would lead to marriage. When she realized that it was not to reach this conclusion, she hid her disappointment behind self-mockery. She seems to have been glad, on the other hand, that Samuel Blackall was unable to get to know her better. When she was an old lady, Cassandra related to her niece the story of her sister holidaying at a resort one summer, where she met a young man with whom she perhaps fell in love. A subsequent meeting was agreed upon – but the next the Austens heard of the young suitor was that he had died. No letters exist from between 1801 and September 1804, which might support the theory that something traumatic happened to Jane Austen around this time and that any letters she wrote would have revealed too much and were thus destroyed by Cassandra. It is, however, known that in December 1802, she did receive – and accepted – a proposal of marriage. It came from Harris Bigg-Wither, the younger brother of her friends Alethea and Catherine. The following morning she told him it had all been a terrible mistake . . . Thereafter she seems to have devoted herself to her writing.

I am almost afraid to tell you how my Irish friend and I behaved. Imagine to yourself everything most profligate and shocking in the way of dancing and sitting down together. I *can* expose myself however, only *once more*, because he leaves the country soon after next Friday, on which day we *are* to have a dance at Ashe after all. He is a very gentlemanlike, good-looking, pleasant young man, I assure you. But as to our having ever met, except at the three last balls, I cannot say much; for he is so excessively laughed at about me at Ashe, that he is ashamed of coming to Steventon, and ran away when we called on Mrs Lefroy a few days ago.

Letter to Cassandra, 9–10 January 1796

He has but *one* fault, which time will, I trust, entirely remove – it is that his morning coat is a great deal too light.

Letter to Cassandra, 9–10 January 1796

Our party to Ashe to-morrow night will consist of Edward Cooper, James (for a ball is nothing without *him*), Buller, who is now staying with us, and I. I look forward with great impatience to it, as I rather expect to receive an offer from my friend in the course of the evening. I shall refuse him, however, unless he promises to give away his white coat.

Letter to Cassandra, 14–15 January 1796

Tell Mary that I make over Mr Heartley and all his estate to her for her sole use and benefit in future, and not only him, but all my other admirers into the bargain wherever she can find them, even the kiss which C. Powlett wanted to give me, as I mean to confine myself in future to Mr Tom Lefroy, for whom I don't care sixpence. Assure her also, as a last and indubitable proof of Warren's indifference to me, that he actually drew that gentleman's picture for me, and delivered it to me without a sigh.

Letter to Cassandra, 14–15 January 1796 (on the 14th)

At length the day is come on which I am to flirt my last with Tom Lefroy, and when you receive this it will be over. My tears flow at the melancholy idea.

Letter to Cassandra, 14–15 January 1796 (on the 15th)

'It would give me particular pleasure to have an opportunity of improving my acquaintance with that family – with a hope of creating to myself a nearer interest' – [*wrote Rev. Samuel Blackall to Mrs Lefroy. But he couldn't . . . Jane Austen was shown his letter and comments:*] This is rational enough; there is less love and more sense in it than sometimes appeared before, and I am very well satisfied. It will all go on exceedingly well, and decline away in a very reasonable manner.

There seems no likelihood of his [Blackall's] coming into Hampshire this Christmas, and it is therefore most probable that our indifference will soon be mutual, unless his regard, which appeared to spring from knowing nothing of me at first, is best supported by never seeing me.

Letter to Cassandra, 17 November 1798

And, years later:

I wonder whether you happened to see Mr Blackall's marriage in the papers last January? *We* did. He was married at Clifton to a Miss Lewis, whose father had been late of Antigua. I should very much like to know what sort of a woman she is. He was a piece of perfection, noisy perfection himself which I always recollect with regard . . . I would wish Miss Lewis to be of a silent turn and rather ignorant, but naturally intelligent and wishing to learn; – fond of cold veal pies, green tea in the afternoon, and a green window blind at night.

Letter to Frank, on HMS Elephant, 3 July 1813

A gentleman had to be introduced to a lady he was not acquainted with before he could ask her to dance with him:

There was one gentleman, an officer of the Cheshire, a very good-looking young man, who, I was told, wanted very much to be introduced to me, but as he did not want it quite enough to take much trouble in effecting it, we never could bring it about.

Letter to Cassandra, 8 January 1799

Jane Austen had running jokes with her family about her marry-ing Rev. John Rawsthorne Papillon (a distant relative of the Knights and rector of Chawton) or the poet George Crabbe.

She [Mrs Knight] may depend upon it that I *will* marry Mr Papillon, whatever may be his reluctance or my own.

Letter to Cassandra, 9 December 1808

I am happy to tell you that Mr Papillon will soon make his offer, probably next Monday, as he returns on Saturday.

Letter to eighteen-year-old Edward Austen-Leigh,
16–17 December 1816

No, I have never seen [news of] the death of Mrs Crabbe. I have only just been making out from one of his prefaces that he probably was married . . . Poor woman! I will comfort *him* as well as I can, but I do not undertake to be good to her children. She had better not leave any.

Letter to Cassandra, 21 December 1813

A Neighbourhood
of Voluntary Spies

FRIENDS AND NEIGHBOURS were a source of delight to Jane Austen – especially those who showed themselves to be in any way absurd or affected; extreme ignorance, too, was a fund of much entertainment – for example when a neighbouring squire asked of her father 'Can you answer that which has been troubling me and my wife: is France in Paris or is Paris in France?' But much of Jane's enjoyment in neighbours and friends was simply in the news and gossip with which they furnished her: who had done what, who had married whom, what so-and-so looked like.

In her descriptions of people she knew or met, there is often, however, a degree of acerbity, especially in those of people at social gatherings, at which, to her mind, those present often displayed themselves at a disadvantage. In 'the elegant stupidity of private parties', Jane Austen found much both to irritate and to amuse her. Her remarks about Miss Armstrong make it clear how exigent she was when it came to other people – it is no wonder that Miss Mitford's friends found her a 'perpendicular, precise, taciturn piece of "single-blessedness"' and 'a poker of whom every one is afraid'.

'For what do we live, but to make sport for our neighbours, and laugh at them in our turn?'

Mr Bennet, Pride and Prejudice, 1813

'In a country like this, where social and literary intercourse is on such a footing, where every man is surrounded by a neighbourhood of voluntary spies.'

Henry Tilney, Northanger Abbey, 1818

Mr Richard Harvey is going to be married; but as it is a great secret and only known to half the neighbourhood, you must not mention it.

Letter to Cassandra, 5 September 1796

Mr Richard Harvey's match is put off, till he has got a better Christian name, of which he has great hopes.

Letter to Cassandra, 15–16 September 1796

(What did JA have against the name Richard? It was perhaps some family joke. In Northanger Abbey, *when describing Catherine's family, she remarks: 'Her father was a clergyman, without being neglected, or poor, and a very respectable man, though his name was Richard – and he had never been handsome.')*

Mr Children's two sons are both going to be married, John and George. They are to have one wife between them, a Miss Holwell, who belongs to the Black Hole at Calcutta.

Letter to Cassandra, 15–16 September 1796

Mrs Hall of Sherbourn was brought to bed yesterday of a dead child, some weeks before she expected, owing to a fright. I suppose she happened unawares to look at her husband.

Letter to Cassandra, 27–8 October 1798

Mrs Portman is not much admired in Dorsetshire; the good-natured world as usual extolled her beauty so highly that all the neighbourhood have had the pleasure of being disappointed.

Letter to Cassandra, 17–18 November 1798

Charles Powlett gave a dance on Thursday, to the great disturbance of all his neighbours, of course, who, you know, take a most lively interest in the state of his finances, and live in hopes of his being soon ruined.

Letter to Cassandra, 1–2 December 1798

I do not want people to be very agreeable, as it saves me the trouble of liking them a great deal.

Letter to Cassandra, 24–6 December 1798

I do not like the Miss Blackstones; indeed, I was always determined not to like them, so there is the less merit in it.

Letter to Cassandra, 8 January 1799

At the bottom of Kingsdown Hill we met a gentleman in a buggy, who, on a minute examination, turned out to be Dr Hall – and Dr Hall in such very deep mourning that either his mother, his wife, or himself must be dead.

Letter to Cassandra, 17 May 1799

I spent Friday evening with the Mapletons, and was obliged to submit to being pleased in spite of my inclination.

Letter to Cassandra, 2 June 1799

Dr Gardiner was married yesterday to Mrs Percy and her three daughters.

Letter to Cassandra, 11 June 1799

The Miss Maitlands are both prettyish . . . with brown skins, large dark eyes, and a good deal of nose. – The General has got the gout, and Mrs Maitland the jaundice. – Miss Debary, Susan and Sally . . . made their appearance, and I was as civil to them as their bad breath would allow me.

Letter to Cassandra, 20–21 November 1800

I am proud to say that I have a very good eye at an adultress, for though repeatedly assured that another in the same party was the *She*, I fixed upon the right one from the first . . . She is not so pretty as I expected. Her face has the same defect of baldness as her sister's and her features not so handsome; – she was highly rouged, and looked rather quietly and contentedly silly than anything else.

Letter to Cassandra, 12–13 May 1801

I cannot anyhow continue to find people agreeable; I respect Mrs Chamberlayne for doing her hair well, but cannot feel a more tender sentiment. Miss Langley is like any other short girl, with a broad nose and wide mouth, fashionable dress and exposed bosom. Adm. Stanhope is a gentleman-like man, but then his legs are too short and his tail too long.

Letter to Cassandra, 12–13 May 1801

I called yesterday morning on Miss Armstrong, and was introduced to her father and mother. Like other young ladies she is considerably genteeler than her parents; Mrs Armstrong sat darning a pair of stockings the whole of my visit. – But I do not mention this at home, lest a warning should act as an example. – We afterwards walked together . . . I do not perceive wit or genius – but she has sense and some degree of taste, and her manners are very engaging. She seems to like people rather too easily.

Letter to Cassandra, 14 September 1804

Unluckily however, I see nothing to be glad of, unless I make it a matter of joy that Mrs Wylmot has another son, and that Lord Lucan has taken a mistress, both of which events are of course joyful to the actors [the participants].

Letter to Cassandra, 8–9 February 1807

We are to have a tiny party here tonight; I hate tiny parties – they force one into constant exertion. – Miss Edwards and her father, Mrs Busby and her nephew Mr Maitland, and Mrs Lillingstone are to be the whole; – and I am prevented from setting my black cap at Mr Maitland by his having a wife and ten children. – My aunt has a very bad cough: do not forget to have heard about *that* when you come . . .

Letter to Cassandra, 21–2 May 1808

PS to the above:

We drink tea tonight with Mrs Busby – I scandalized her nephew cruelly; he has but three children instead of ten.

I shall not tell you anything more of William Digweed's china, as your silence on the subject makes you unworthy of it.

Letter to Cassandra, 27–8 December 1808

Mr Digweed has used us basely. Handsome is as handsome does; he is therefore a very ill-looking man.

Letter to Cassandra, 24 January 1813

On the Peninsular War:

How horrible it is to have so many people killed! And what a blessing that one cares for none of them!

Letter to Cassandra, 31 May 1811

If Mrs Freeman is anywhere above ground give my best compliments to her.

Letter to Cassandra, 9 February 1813

He seems a very harmless sort of young man, nothing to like or dislike in him – goes out shooting or hunting with the two others all the morning, and plays at whist and makes queer faces in the evening.

Letter to Cassandra, 23–4 September 1813

(The young man in question was Wadham Knatchbull, then aged eighteen or nineteen.)

Only think of Mrs Holder's being dead! Poor woman, she has done the only thing in the world she could possibly do to make one cease to abuse her.

Letter to Cassandra, 14–15 October 1813

We have got rid of Mr R. Mascall, however. I did not like *him* either. He talks too much, and is conceited, besides having a vulgarly shaped mouth.

Letter to Cassandra, 14–15 October 1813

Of one Mrs Tilson:

Poor woman! how can she honestly be breeding again?

Letter to Cassandra, 1–2 October 1808

The Webbs are really gone! When I saw the waggons at the door, and thought of all the trouble they must have in moving, I began to reproach myself for not having liked them better – but since the waggons have disappeared my conscience has been closed again, and I am excessively glad they are gone.

Letter to Anna Austen, 28 September 1814

On their friend Mrs Deedes giving birth to another child:

I would recommend to her and Mr D. the simple regimen of separate rooms.

Letter to Fanny Knight, 20–1 February 1817

Vanity Working on a Weak Head:

The Absurdity of
Self-Regard
and Affectation

M UCH OF THE COMEDY in Jane Austen revolves around absurdity and affectation; and certainly her comic characters all have a good helping of some absurd characteristic or other. Sometimes the portrait is affectionate – Mr Woodhouse's old-maidish fussiness – but usually it is a great deal fiercer – the stupid interfering snobbery of Lady Catherine de Bourgh, the self-satisfied obsequiousness of Mr Collins, the vanity of Sir Walter Elliot who turns to his day's equivalent of *Burke's Peerage* to read about himself.

THE VAIN AND AFFECTED

Their vanity was in such good order that they seemed to be quite free from it.

Mansfield Park, 1814

Vanity was the beginning and the end of Sir Walter Elliot's character; vanity of person and of situation.

Persuasion, 1818

'Vanity working on a weak head, produces every sort of mischief.'

MR KNIGHTLEY, *Emma*, 1816

She had not been brought up . . . to know to how many idle assertions and impudent falsehoods the excess of vanity will lead.

Northanger Abbey, 1818

It was a struggle between propriety and vanity; but vanity got the better.

Persuasion, 1818

'It is very often nothing but our own vanity that deceives us. Women fancy admiration means more than it does.'

JANE BENNET, *Pride and Prejudice*, 1813

Sir Walter Elliot . . . was a man who, for his own amusement, never took up any book but the Baronetage; there he found occupation for an idle hour, and consolation in a distressed one; there his faculties were roused into admiration and respect, by contemplating the limited remnant of the earliest patents; there any unwelcome sensations, arising from domestic affairs changed naturally into pity and contempt as he turned over the almost endless creations of the last century; and there, if every other leaf were powerless, he could read his own history with an interest which never failed.

Persuasion, 1818

Sir Walter was happiest with titles:

A Mr (save, perhaps, some half dozen in the nation,) always needs a note of explanation.

Persuasion, 1818

'A man . . . must have a very good opinion of himself when he asks people to leave their own fireside, and encounter such a day as this, for the sake of coming to see him. He must think himself a most agreeable fellow; I could not do such a thing. It is the greatest absurdity.'

MR JOHN KNIGHTLEY, *Emma*, 1816

Sir Edward's great object in life was to be seductive. – With such personal advantages as he knew himself to possess, and such talents as he did also give himself credit for, he regarded it as his duty. – He felt that he was formed to be a dangerous man – quite in the line of the Lovelaces. – The very name of 'Sir Edward', he thought, carried some degree of fascination with it.

Sanditon, 1817

Mrs Breton called here on Saturday. I never saw her before. She is a large, ungenteel woman, with self-satisfied and would-be elegant manners.

Letter to Cassandra, 11–12 October 1813

Dr Breton . . . his wife amuses me very much with her affected refinement and elegance.

Letter to Cassandra, 6–7 November 1813

THE SNOBBISH

'I am happy on every occasion to offer those little delicate compliments which are always acceptable to ladies. I have more than once observed to Lady Catherine that her charming daughter seemed born to be a duchess, and that the most elevated rank, instead of giving her consequence, would be adorned by her. These are the kind of little things which please her ladyship, and it is a sort of attention which I conceive myself peculiarly bound to pay.'

'You judge very properly,' said Mr Bennet; 'and it is happy for you that you possess the talent of flattering with delicacy. May I ask whether these pleasing attentions proceed from the impulse of the moment, or are the result of previous study?'

'They arise chiefly from what is passing at the time, and though I sometimes amuse myself with suggesting and arranging such little elegant compliments as may be adapted to ordinary occasions, I always wish to give them as unstudied an air as possible.'

Mr Bennet's expectations were fully answered. His cousin was as absurd as he had hoped; and he listened to him with the keenest enjoyment.

Pride and Prejudice, 1813

There was little to be done but to hear Lady Catherine talk, which she did without any intermission till coffee came in,

delivering her opinion on every subject in so decisive a manner, as proved that she was not used to have her judgment
controverted.

Pride and Prejudice, 1813

*Elizabeth Bennet enjoyed overhearing the snobbish Miss Bingley
making something of a fool of herself while trying to ingratiate
herself with Mr Darcy in this exchange:*

'How delighted Miss Darcy will be to receive such a letter!'
  He made no answer.
  'You write uncommonly fast.'
  'You are mistaken; I write rather slowly.'
  'How many letters you must have occasion to write in the
course of a year! Letters of business, too! How odious I
should think them!'
  'It is fortunate, then, that they fall to my lot instead of to
yours.'
  'Pray tell your sister that I long to see her.'
  'I have already told her so once, by your desire.'
  'I am afraid you do not like your pen. Let me mend it for
you. I mend pens remarkably well.'
  'Thank you – but I always mend my own.'
  'How can you contrive to write so even?'
  He was silent.
  'Tell your sister I am delighted to hear of her improvement
on the harp; and pray let her know that I am quite in raptures
with her beautiful little design for a table, and I think it
infinitely superior to Miss Grantley's.'
  'Will you give me leave to defer your raptures till I write
again? At present I have not room to do them justice.'

Pride and Prejudice, 1813

She had prejudices on the side of ancestry; she had a value for rank and consequence, which blinded her a little to the faults of those who possessed them.

Persuasion, 1818, of Lady Russell

The rude and the absurd

Lady Middleton could no longer endure such a conversation, and therefore exerted herself to ask Mr Palmer if there was any news in the paper.

'No, none at all,' he replied, and read on.

Sense and Sensibility, 1811

'My love, you contradict every body,' said his wife with her usual laugh. 'Do you know that you are quite rude?'

'I did not know I contradicted any body in calling your mother ill-bred.'

Sense and Sensibility, 1811

His mother-in-law was, however, unperturbed; she had an answer:

'Ay, you may abuse me as you please . . . you have taken Charlotte off my hands, and cannot give her back again. So there I have the whip hand of you.'

Still Mrs Norris was at intervals urging something different; and in the most interesting moment of his passage to England, when the alarm of a French privateer was at the height, she burst through his recital with the proposal of soup. 'Sure, my dear Sir Thomas, a basin of soup would be a much better thing for you than tea. Do have a basin of soup.'

Persuasion, 1818

AND THE ARROGANT AND SELF-CENTRED

'Nothing is more deceitful than the appearance of humility. It is often only carelessness of opinion, and sometimes an indirect boast.'

MR DARCY, *Pride and Prejudice*, 1813

'It is very difficult for the prosperous to be humble.'

FRANK CHURCHILL, *Emma*, 1816

'Selfishness must always be forgiven, you know, because there is no hope of a cure.'

MARY CRAWFORD, *Mansfield Park*, 1814

'I dare say I shall catch it; and my sore-throats, you know, are always worse than anybody's.'

MARY MUSGRAVE, *Persuasion*, 1818

'People who suffer as I do from nervous complaints can have no great inclination for talking. Nobody can tell what I suffer! But it is always so. Those who do not complain are never pitied.'

Mrs Bennet, *Pride and Prejudice*, 1813

'You take delight in vexing me. You have no compassion on my poor nerves.'

'You mistake me, my dear. I have a high respect for your nerves. They are my old friends. I have heard you mention them with consideration these twenty years at least.'

Mr and Mrs Bennet, *Pride and Prejudice*, 1813

The Dissipations of London, the Luxuries of Bath

J ANE AUSTEN'S TRAVELS were limited. She never ventured abroad, and generally confined her journeys to visiting friends and relatives, either locally in Hampshire, or south of London. At one time the family lived in Bath – in Jane Austen's day a fashionable place for the taking of waters from its famous spa. She occasionally went to London to go to the theatre with family or friends, but found it somewhat flat – rather than a 'scene of dissipation and vice'. Her final days were spent in Winchester.

'Beware of the insipid vanities and idle dissipations of the metropolis of England; Beware of the unmeaning luxuries of Bath and of the stinking fish of Southampton.'

'Alas! (exclaimed I) how am I to avoid those evils I shall never be exposed to? What probability is there of my ever tasting the dissipations of London, the luxuries of Bath, or the stinking fish of Southampton? I who am doomed to waste my Days of Youth and Beauty in an humble cottage in the Vale of Uske.'

LAURA, *Love and Freindship*, 1790

'One has not great hopes from Birmingham. I always say there is something direful in the sound.'

MRS ELTON, *Emma*, 1816

'Oh! Who can ever be tired of Bath?'

. . . Catherine was so hopeful a scholar that when they gained the top of Beechen Cliff, she voluntarily rejected the whole city of Bath as unworthy to make part of a landscape.

Northanger Abbey, 1818

The first view of Bath in fine weather does not answer my expectations; I think I see more distinctly through rain. The sun was got behind everything, and the appearance of the place from the top of Kingsdown was all vapour, shadow, smoke, and confusion.

Letter to Cassandra, 5–6 May 1801

'Every five years, one hears of some new place or other starting up by the sea and growing the fashion. How they can half of them be filled is the wonder! Where people can be found with money and time to go to them!'

MR HEYWOOD, *Sanditon*, 1817

'We do not look in great cities for our best morality.'

EDMUND BERTRAM, *Mansfield Park*, 1814

The language of London is flat.

Letter to Martha Lloyd, 2 September 1814

'The truth is, that in London it is always a sickly season. Nobody is healthy in London, nobody can be.'

Mr Woodhouse, Emma, 1816

Miss Middleton seems very happy, but has not beauty enough to figure in London.

Letter to Cassandra, 25 April 1811

On arriving in London:

Here I am once more in this scene of dissipation and vice, and I begin already to find my morals corrupted.

Letter to Cassandra, 23 August 1796

'Wherever you are you should always be contented, but especially at home, because there you must spend the most of your time.' I did not quite like, at breakfast, to hear you talk so much about the French bread at Northanger.'

Mrs Morland, Northanger Abbey, 1818

A Fine Family

IT WOULD BE FAIR to say that Jane Austen's family meant the world to her, especially, of course, her sister Cassandra, but her brothers too – Henry, who helped her get her books published (and was so proud of her he blabbed to the physician he shared with the Prince Regent), Frank, Charles, all of them; her nephews and nieces, to whom she gave sound literary advice – and love advice. She wasn't above the odd sharp comment about Anna's behaviour, or a spot of stirring – or at least the announced intention of doing a bit of stirring by telling the groom-to-be's relatives that his bride was a touch mad, but that so was he . . .

'Nobody, who has not been in the interior of a family, can say what the difficulties of any individual of that family may be.'

EMMA, *Emma*, 1816

Miss Frances married, in the common phrase, to disoblige her family, and by fixing on a lieutenant of marines, without education, fortune, or connexions, did it very thoroughly.

Mansfield Park, 1814

'Family squabbling is the greatest evil of all, and we had better do anything than be altogether by the ears.'

EDMUND BERTRAM, *Mansfield Park*, 1814

Children of the same family, the same blood, with the same first associations and habits, have some means of enjoyment in their power, which no subsequent connexions can supply.

Mansfield Park, 1814

A family of ten children will be always called a fine family, where there are heads and arms and legs enough for the number.

Northanger Abbey, 1818

I shall think with tenderness and delight on his beautiful and smiling countenance and interesting manner, until a few years have turned him into an ungovernable, ungracious fellow.

Letter to Cassandra, on one of their nephews,
27–8 October 1798

I believe I never told you that Mrs Coulthard and Anne, late of Manydown, are both dead, and both died in childbed. We have not regaled Mary with this news.

Letter to Cassandra, 17–18 November 1798

(Mary was their brother James's very pregnant wife: James-Edward was safely born that very day, 'both mother and child doing well', though Jane was a bit disparaging about Mary: '. . . not tidy enough in appearance; she has no dressing-gown to sit up in'. History does not relate whether Mary had acquired a dressing-gown by the time of her daughter Caroline's birth in 1805.)

I expected to have heard from you this morning, but no letter is come. I shall not take the trouble of announcing to you any more of Mary's children, if, instead of thanking me for the intelligence, you always sit down and write to James. I am sure nobody can desire your letters so much as I do, and I don't think anybody deserves them so well.

Letter to Cassandra, 25 November 1798

Early in 1801 the Austen family moved to Bath; Jane seems to have found the moving plans and especially her family's suggestions as to the disposal of her belongings somewhat irksome.

My mother looks forward with as much certainty as you can do to our keeping two maids . . . We plan having a steady cook and a young, giddy housemaid, with a sedate, middle-aged man, who is to undertake the double office of husband to the former and sweetheart to the latter. No children, of course, to be allowed on either side.

Letter to Cassandra, 3–5 January 1801

You are very kind in planning presents for me to make, and my mother has shown me exactly the same attention; but as I do not choose to have generosity dictated to me, I shall not resolve on giving my cabinet to Anna till the first thought of it has been my own.

Letter to Cassandra, 8–9 January 1801

You will have a great deal of unreserved discourse with Mrs K., I dare say, upon this subject, as well as upon many other of our family matters. Abuse everybody but me.

Letter to Cassandra, 7–8 January 1807

Cousin Fanny Austen's match is quite news, and I am sorry she has behaved so ill. There is some comfort to *us* in her misconduct, that we have not a congratulatory letter to write.

Letter to Cassandra, 30 June–1 July 1808

Sometimes, she felt obliged to say something about Cassandra's spelling:

I tell you everything, and it is unknown the mysteries you conceal from me; and, to add to the rest, you persevere in giving a final *e* to invalid, thereby putting it out of one's power to suppose Mrs E. Leigh, even for a moment, a veteran soldier.

Letter to Cassandra, 24 January 1809

The Portsmouth paper gave a melancholy history of a poor mad woman, escaped from confinement, who said her husband and daughter, of the name of Payne, lived at Ashford, in Kent. Do you own them?

Letter to Cassandra, 24 January 1809

A lady, without a family, was the very best preserver of furniture in the world.

Persuasion, 1818

I give you joy of our new nephew, and hope if he ever comes to be hanged it will not be till we are too old to care about it.

Letter to Cassandra, 25 April 1811

(On the birth of Henry Edgar to their brother Frank's wife, also called Mary.)

I take it for granted that Mary has told you of Anna's engagement to Ben Lefroy. It came upon us without much preparation; – at the same time, there was *that* about her which kept us in a constant preparation for something.

Letter to Frank, 25 September 1813

My dearest Aunt Cass,
I have just asked Aunt Jane to let me write a little in her letter, but she does not like it, so I won't – good-bye.

Fanny Knight in JA's Letter to Cassandra, 11–12 October 1813

I am to meet Mrs Harrison, and we are to talk about Ben and Anna. 'My dear Mrs Harrison,' I shall say, 'I am afraid the young man has some of your family madness, and though there often appears to be something of madness in Anna too, I think she inherits more of it from her mother's family than from ours.' That is what I shall say, and I think she will find it difficult to answer me.

Letter to Cassandra, 3 November 1813

Mrs F. A. seldom either looks or appears quite well. Little Embryo is troublesome, I suppose.

Letter to Cassandra, 8-9 September 1814

(Mrs F.A. was Frank's wife, Mary.)

I rather imagine indeed that nieces are seldom chosen but out of compliment to some aunt or another.

Letter to Anna Lefroy (Austen), 30 November 1814

I am glad you recollected to mention your being come home. My heart began to sink within me when I had got so far through your letter without its being mentioned. I was dreadfully afraid that you might be detained at Winchester by severe illness, confined to your bed perhaps, and quite unable to hold a pen, and only dating from Steventon in order, with a mistaken sort of tenderness, to deceive me. But now I have no doubt of your being at home. I am sure you would not say it so seriously unless it actually were so. We saw a countless number of post-chaises full of boys pass by yesterday morning – full of future heroes, legislators, fools, and villains. You have never thanked me for my last letter, which went by the cheese. I cannot bear not to be thanked. You will not pay us a visit yet of course; we must not think of it.

Letter to Edward Austen-Leigh, 9 July 1816

Now that you are become an aunt, you are a person of some consequence and must excite great interest whatever you do. I have always maintained the importance of aunts as much as possible, and I am sure of your doing the same now.

Letter to ten-year-old Caroline Austen, 30 October 1815

(On the occasion of the birth of Anna Lefroy's first child)

I give you joy of having left Winchester. Now you may own how miserable you were there; now it will gradually all come out, your crimes and your miseries — how often you went up by the Mail to London and threw away fifty guineas at a tavern, and how often you were on the point of hanging yourself, restrained only, as some ill-natured aspersion upon poor old Winton has it, by the want of a tree within some miles of the city.

Letter to Edward Austen-Leigh, 16–17 December 1816

The pianoforte often talks of you; – in various keys, tunes and expressions I allow – but be it lesson or country dance, sonata or waltz, *you* really its constant theme.

Letter to twelve-year-old Caroline Austen, 23 January 1817

Ben and Anna walked here . . . and she looked so pretty, it was quite a pleasure to see her, so young and so blooming, and so innocent, as if she had never had a wicked thought in her life, which yet one has some reason to suppose she must have had, if we believe the doctrine of original sin or if we remember the events of her girlish days.

Letter to Fanny Knight, 20–1 February 1817

(JA is probably alluding to Anna's engagement to Michael Terry when she was very young and headstrong.)

Anna has not a chance of escape; her husband called here the other day, and said she was *pretty* well but not *equal* to so long a walk; she *must come in* her *donkey carriage*. Poor Animal, she will be worn out before she is thirty. – I am very sorry for her. Mrs Clement too is in that way again. I am quite tired of so many children. – Mrs Benn has a 13th.

Letter to Fanny Knight, 23–5 March 1817

(Anna Lefroy had already had two children and was believed to be expecting a third; she had however been ill, and had possibly miscarried – her third child was not born until 1818.)

Of Sterling Insignificance

As AN AUTHOR Jane Austen had a most enviable genius for brevity – a short sentence can convey all that needs to be known about a character, whether in her novels or in her letters. Unlike Mrs Ferrars in *Sense and Sensibility*, however, with her, few words did not indicate few ideas. A simple juxtaposition of words can be enough – 'querulous serenity', 'sterling insignificance'. And who has not met people like Sir Thomas Champneys, clearly a man of double standards, or like Mrs Bennet, stupid and full of complaints, or Mrs Digweed, vulnerable and lovable, if not very bright?

Jane Austen appreciated, too, that a possibly mischievous brevity can be the best way to convey bad news, at least about trees . . .

Referring to the eponymous – and most unprincipled – Lady Susan:

She had nothing against her but her husband and her conscience.

Lady Susan, ?1793–5

'People who suffer as I do from nervous complaints can have no great inclination for talking . . .' She [Mrs Bennet] talked on.

Pride and Prejudice, 1813

I looked at Sir Thomas Champneys and thought of poor Rosalie; I looked at his daughter, and thought her a queer animal with a white neck.

Letter to Cassandra, 20–21 November 1800

Mr Robert Mascall . . . eats a great deal of butter.

Letter to Cassandra, 11–12 October 1813

[Mr Lushington, MP, MF] is quite an MP – very smiling, with an exceeding good address, and readiness of language . . . I dare say he is ambitious and insincere.

Letter to Cassandra, 14–15 October 1813

[Mrs Bennet] was a woman of mean understanding, little information, and uncertain temper.

Pride and Prejudice, 1813

A person and face, of strong, natural, sterling insignificance.

Sense and Sensibility, 1811

Dear Mrs Digweed! – I cannot bear that she should not be foolishly happy after a ball.

Letter to Cassandra, 11–12 October 1813

Of John Murray, JA's last publisher:

He is a rogue of course, but a civil one.

> Letter to Cassandra, 17–18 October 1815

Mrs Bennet was restored to her usual querulous serenity.

> *Pride and Prejudice*, 1813

[Mrs Ferrars] was not a woman of many words; for, unlike people in general, she proportioned them to the number of her ideas.

> *Sense and Sensibility*, 1811

He knew her illnesses; they never occurred but for her own convenience.

> *Emma*, 1816

(Frank Churchill had been summoned to the bedside of his aunt.)

[Miss Bates] enjoyed a most uncommon degree of popularity for a woman neither young, handsome, rich, nor married.

> *Emma*, 1816

Mrs Norris was one of those well-meaning people who are always doing mistaken and very disagreeable things.

Mansfield Park, 1814

'Mr Wickham is blessed with such happy manners as may ensure his making friends: whether he may be equally capable of retaining them is less certain.'

Elizabeth Bennet, *Pride and Prejudice*, 1813

I will not say that your mulberry-trees are dead, but I am afraid they are not alive.

Letter to Cassandra, 31 May 1811

One Half Cannot
Understand the Other:
Observations General
and Particular

ALTHOUGH some of Jane Austen's characters' comments tell the reader more about the character's opinion – Mary Crawford's spiel against clergymen, for example – than about Jane Austen's own views, there is wisdom to be found as well as wit in her novels. That one half of the world cannot understand the pleasures of the other holds as true today as it did then, and on many levels – from being tossed up and down (the original pleasure which horrified Mr Woodhouse), to state and international affairs. There is the thoughtful self-doubt of Colonel Brandon, the witty but also thoughtful compliment Henry Tilney pays Catherine; and how true that we quickly justify what we like, that when everybody holds an opinion it must be correct – and that surprises are inconvenient!

'One half of the world cannot understand the pleasures of the other.'

EMMA, *Emma*, 1816

'Why not seize the pleasure at once? How often is happiness destroyed by preparation, foolish preparation!'

FRANK CHURCHILL, *Emma*, 1816

'The pleasantness of an employment does not always evince its propriety.'

ELINOR DASHWOOD, *Sense and Sensibility*, 1811

'It is particularly incumbent on those who never change their opinion to be secure of judging properly at first.'

ELIZABETH BENNET, Pride and Prejudice, 1813

'The more I see of the world, the more am I dissatisfied with it; and every day confirms my belief of the inconsistency of all human characters, and of the little dependence that can be placed on the appearance of either merit or sense.'

ELIZABETH BENNET, Pride and Prejudice, 1813

Seldom, very seldom, does complete truth belong to any human disclosure; seldom can it happen that something is not a little disguised, or a little mistaken; but where, as in this case, though the conduct is mistaken, the feelings are not, it may not be very material.

Emma, 1816

To look almost pretty is an acquisition of higher delight to a girl who has been looking plain the first fifteen years of her life than a beauty from her cradle can ever receive.

Northanger Abbey, 1818

'Think only of the past as its remembrance gives you pleasure.'

ELIZABETH BENNET, Pride and Prejudice, 1813

[The typical clergyman] 'is very sincere in preferring an income ready made, to the trouble of working for one; and has the best intentions of doing nothing all the rest of his days but eat, drink, and grow fat. It is indolence, Mr Bertram, indeed. Indolence and love of ease; a want of all laudable ambition, of taste for good company, or of inclination to take the trouble of being agreeable, which make men clergymen. A clergyman has nothing to do but be slovenly and selfish – read the news-paper, watch the weather, and quarrel with his wife. His curate does all the work, and the business of his own life is to dine.'

MARY CRAWFORD, *Mansfield Park*, 1814

'I do not know whether it ought to be so, but certainly silly things do cease to be silly if they are done by sensible people in an impudent way. Wickedness is always wickedness, but folly is not always folly. – It depends upon the character of those who handle it.'

EMMA, *Emma*, 1816

'But your mind is warped by an innate principle of general integrity, and therefore not accessible to the cool reasonings of family partiality, or a desire of revenge.'

HENRY TILNEY, *Northanger Abbey*, 1818

How quick come the reasons for approving what we like!

Persuasion, 1818

Where people wish to attach, they should always be ignorant. To come with a well-informed mind is to come with an inability of administering to the vanity of others, which a sensible person would always wish to avoid. A woman especially, if she have the misfortune of knowing anything, should conceal it as well as she can.

Northanger Abbey, 1818

The real evils, indeed, of Emma's situation were the power of having rather too much her own way, and a disposition to think a little too well of herself.

Emma, 1816

'It is the worst evil of too yielding and indecisive a character, that no influence over it can be depended on. You are never sure of a good impression being durable; everybody may sway it. Let those who would be happy be firm.'

Captain Wentworth, *Persuasion*, 1818

'Where an opinion is general, it is usually correct.'

Mary Crawford, *Mansfield Park*, 1814

Emma denied none of it aloud, and agreed to none of it in private.

Emma, 1816

'It is a most repulsive quality, indeed. Oftentimes very convenient, no doubt, but never pleasing. There is safety in reserve, but no attraction. One cannot love a reserved person.'

FRANK CHURCHILL, Emma, 1816

'Surprises are foolish things. The pleasure is not enhanced, and the inconvenience is often considerable.'

MR KNIGHTLEY, Emma, 1816

'Where so many hours have been spent in convincing myself that I am right, is there not some reason to fear I may be wrong?'

COLONEL BRANDON, Sense and Sensibility, 1811

'The memory is sometimes so retentive, so serviceable, so obedient; at others, so bewildered and so weak; and at others again, so tyrannic, so beyond control! We are, to be sure, a miracle every way; but our powers of recollecting and of forgetting do seem peculiarly past finding out.'

FANNY, Mansfield Park, 1814

'It is not time or opportunity that is to determine intimacy; – It is disposition alone. Seven years would be insufficient to make some people acquainted with each other, and seven days are more than enough for others.'

MARIANNE DASHWOOD, Sense and Sensibility, 1811

An occasional memento of past folly, however painful, might not be without use.

Northanger Abbey, 1818

There are people, who the more you do for them, the less they will do for themselves.

Emma, 1816

'To be always firm must be to be often obstinate.'

Henry Tilney, *Northanger Abbey*, 1818

She felt she was in the greatest danger of being exquisitely happy, while so many were miserable.

Mansfield Park, 1814

'It will be a bitter pill to her; that is, like other bitter pills, it will have two moments' ill-flavour, and then be swallowed and forgotten.'

Henry Crawford, *Mansfield Park*, 1814

'Our pleasures in this world are always to be paid for.'

Henry Tilney, *Northanger Abbey*, 1818

. . . in that inconvenient tone of voice which was perfectly audible while it pretended to be a whisper.

Persuasion, 1818

'The kind of man . . . whom every body speaks well of, and nobody cares about; whom all are delighted to see, and nobody remembers to talk to.'

Willoughby, *Sense and Sensibility*, 1811

With such a reward [*sugar plums*] for her tears, the child was too wise to cease crying.

Sense and Sensibility, 1811

The old, well-established grievance of duty against will, parent against child.

Persuasion, 1818

From politics, it was an easy step to silence.

Northanger Abbey, 1818

After long thought and much perplexity, to be very brief was all that she could determine on with any confidence of safety.

Northanger Abbey, 1818

Mr Wickham, who had charmed everybody with his pleasant conversation, graceful manners and good looks, was discovered to be a dishonest rascal interested primarily in money . . . He was declared to be in debt to every tradesman in the place, and his intrigues, all honoured with the title of seduction, had been extended into every tradesman's family. Everybody declared that he was the wickedest young man in the world; and everybody began to find out, that they had always distrusted the appearance of his goodness.

Pride and Prejudice, 1813

'A man who has nothing to do with his own time has no conscience in his intrusion on that of others.'

Marianne Dashwood, *Sense and Sensibility*, 1811

Like half the rest of the world, if more than half there be that are clever and good, Marianne, with excellent abilities and an excellent disposition, was neither reasonable nor candid. She expected from other people the same opinions and feelings as her own, and she judged of their motives by the immediate effect of their actions on herself.

Sense and Sensibility, 1811

'I am particularly unlucky in meeting with a person so well able to expose my real character, in a part of the world, where I had hoped to pass myself off with some degree of credit.'

Elizabeth Bennet, *Pride and Prejudice*, 1813

I Am a Very Good Housekeeper

I N HER LETTERS Jane Austen was rarely serious about her-self – what we learn is that she pretended to be vain, was not especially interested in sponge cakes, was probably worried about growing old – and didn't want to worry her family with accounts of her illness . . .

My mother desires me to tell you that I am a very good housekeeper, which I have no reluctance in doing, because I really think it my peculiar excellence, and for this reason – I always take care to provide such things as please my own appetite, which I consider as the chief merit in housekeeping.

Letter to Cassandra, 17–18 November 1798

You deserve a longer letter than this; but it is my unhappy fate seldom to treat people so well as they deserve.

Letter to Cassandra, 24–6 December 1798

You express so little anxiety about my being murdered under Ash Park Copse by Mrs Hulbert's servant, that I have a great mind not to tell you whether I was or not.

Letter to Cassandra, 8–9 January 1799

Your letter is come; it came indeed twelve lines ago, but I could not stop to acknowledge it before, and I am glad it did not arrive till I had completed my first sentence, because the sentence had been made since yesterday, and I think forms a very good beginning.

Letter to Cassandra, 1 November 1800

(She had begun her letter: 'You have written I am sure, though I have received no letter from you since your leaving London; – the post, and not yourself, must have been unpunctual.')

Expect a most agreeable letter, for not being overburdened with subject (having nothing at all to say), I shall have no check to my genius from beginning to end.

Letter to Cassandra, 21 January 1801

I am forced to be abusive for want of subject, having really nothing to say.

Letter to Cassandra, 20–2 February 1807

You know how interesting the purchase of a sponge-cake is to me.

Letter to Cassandra, 15 June 1808

Our ball was rather more amusing than I expected . . . The melancholy part was, to see so many dozen young women standing by without partners, and each of them with two ugly naked shoulders! It was the same room in which we danced fifteen years ago! I thought it all over, and in spite of the shame of being so much older, felt with thankfulness that I was quite as happy now as then.

Letter to Cassandra, 9 December 1808

[I] am very well satisfied with his notice of me – 'A pleasing looking young woman' – that must do; one cannot pretend to anything better now; thankful to have it continued a few years longer!

Letter to Cassandra, 30 April 1811

I bought a concert ticket and a sprig of flowers for my old age.

Letter to Cassandra, 3 November 1813

(JA wasn't yet thirty-eight!)

By the bye, as I must leave off being young, I find many douceurs in being a sort of chaperon for I am put on the sofa near the fire and can drink as much wine as I like.

Letter to Cassandra, 6 November 1813

I am sorry my mother has been suffering, and am afraid this exquisite weather is too good to agree with her. I enjoy it all over me, from top to toe, from right to left, longitudinally, perpendicularly, diagonally; and I cannot but selfishly hope we are to have it last till Christmas – nice, unwholesome, unseasonable, relaxing, close, muggy weather.

Letter to Cassandra, 2 December 1815

. . . such weather as gives one little temptation to be out. It is really too bad, and has been too bad for a long time, much worse than any one *can* bear, and I begin to think it will never be fine again. This is a *finesse* of mine, for I have often observed that if one writes about the weather, it is generally completely changed before the letter is read.

Letter to Edward Austen-Leigh, 9 July 1816

I am considerably better now and am recovering my looks a little, which have been bad enough – black and white, and every wrong colour. I must not depend upon being ever very blooming again. Sickness is a dangerous indulgence at my time of life.

Letter to Fanny Knight, 23–5 March 1817

Jane Austen was by now very ill with what many believe to have been Addison's disease – a feature of this disease is increased pigmentation. After a long battle with the illness, throughout which she did her best to make light of her troubles, she died early in the morning of 18 July 1817, Cassandra having kept an almost constant vigil at her bedside.